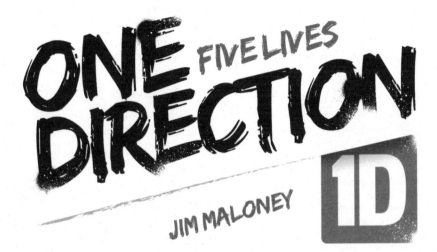

ONE FIVE LIVES DIRECTION 1D

JIM MALONEY

OMNIBUS PRESS

London / New York / Paris / Sydney / Copenhagen / Berlin / Madrid / Tokyo

**Exclusive Distributors**
Music Sales Limited,
14/15 Berners Street,
London, W1T 3LJ.

**Music Sales Corporation**
180 Madison Avenue, 24th Floor,
New York, NY 10016,
USA.

**Macmillan Distribution Services**
56 Parkwest Drive,
Derrimut, Vic 3030,
Australia.

Every effort has been made to trace the copyright holders of the photographs in this book but one or
two were unreachable. We would be grateful if the photographers concerned would contact us.

Typeset by Phoenix Photosetting, Chatham, Kent
Printed in the EU

A catalogue record for this book is available from the British Library.

Visit Omnibus Press on the web at www.omnibuspress.com

# Contents

# Introduction

They're going 'crazy, crazy, crazy', as they joyously declared in their anthem 'Live While We're Young'. There's little doubt about that: normal life has been blown away as these boys travel around the world, causing near-hysteria amongst fans – and a headache for the police and security who are valiantly trying to keep control.

In an astonishingly short space of time – they were only formed towards the end of 2010 – five teenage boys have gone from being just average normal kids, to worldwide stars. Living life while they're young is no idle boast for these boys: they have taken life by the neck and given it a good shaking!

Harry, Liam, Louis, Niall and Zayn have been going in One Direction only since the band was formed. But the speed and magnitude of their success has amazed them and their influential management team as much as anyone else.

Their debut album, *Up All Night*, shot to the top of the charts in the UK and across the Atlantic in America. Their debut single, 'What Makes You Beautiful', was number one in the UK and made the highest entry for a British act in the US singles charts for 14 years. What makes this even more remarkable is that over 100,000 copies were downloaded before it was even played on US radio stations. Subsequent singles and albums have topped the charts all over the world. At the prestigious Brit Awards in February 2012, 'What Makes You Beautiful' was voted best single.

So how did it all happen? Well, it springs from failure... of sorts. Reaching the latter stages of the biggest television talent show in the world was a tremendous achievement for Harry, Liam, Louis, Niall and Zayn as individual singers. Not only did it turn them into local celebrities in their hometowns, it raised their profile further afield. *The X Factor* was the most watched TV show in the UK, seen by millions. But, having come so far in the competition, things looked like they had come to an end when each of them failed to make it to the finals.

Then came the crucial turning point. The show's judges, Simon Cowell, Louis Walsh and Nicole Scherzinger, have all claimed to be the one to first suggest putting the five 'rejects' into a band. It was to be one of the best decisions in the history of pop music – at least in terms of their subsequent, record-breaking international success.

No one back then could have dreamt of what was to come. The five boys had just three weeks in which to form themselves into a band. Harmonising and the apportioning of lines to sing was all new to them, as was the concept of five individuals' hopes and aspirations coming together as one. They barely knew each other and it could quite easily have gone disastrously wrong, but just how right they got it would take everyone by surprise. Simon Cowell said that the moment they first sang in front of him as a group was when he knew they had something special.

Having progressed to the live finals, One Direction's high-energy weekly performances were a highlight for many. The screams from the audience were louder for them than for any other act and became increasingly audible each week. The judges loved them too. They looked and sounded right for a boy band, their energy and enthusiasm were as infectious as the obvious fun they were having. It was feel-good time when they were onstage, and their professionalism, commitment and all-round niceness backstage was much noticed and appreciated.

One Direction were fortunate in that all five of them got on so well together. They had come from different parts of the UK and Ireland, but found that they had much in common – the main thing being that they were just normal, unpretentious lads. There was certainly no diva in this group, and their friendship was the bedrock of their success.

But they did not win *The X Factor*. Neither were they runners-up. After finishing third, they knew that they wanted to stay together as a band but were unsure of what the future held for them. That was settled the very next day, when Simon gave them a record deal. What happened next was a whirlwind that turned into a tornado and roared its way around the world, as country after country was engulfed. And it's still blowing.

Just how they managed to make such an impact everywhere they went is a combination of factors – not least *The X Factor*, Simon Cowell and his management team, the boys' individual personalities and, vitally, the power of social media.

When the boys first arrived in America at the end of January 2011, they were startled by the fans who gathered to greet them at LA Airport. Some were holding a banner with 'One Direction' written on it; although their records had not yet been played in the USA, many knew about them via clips of their *X Factor* performances on YouTube and the boys' direct line to fans on Twitter. Their regular tweets about what they were doing – from promotional tours to eating toast – were avidly read by a fast-growing army of fans. Combined with slick management and impeccable timing, it resulted in a ready-made fanbase around the world. They did not have to go out and conquer as performers had traditionally done before them. Rather, their fans were already waiting for them. Social media had never broken an act quite like this before.

A familiar format evolved: a short promotional 'meet and greet' tour in major cities in the UK, Europe, North America and, later, other regions of the world, would warm up the fans, spread the word about One Direction and pave the way for their return a few months later, when they would perform there. Having laid the foundation, the crowd that greeted them on their second visit would be even bigger than before and their wide-eyed fans would follow them around, chanting their names outside their hotel.

A second visit to the US, in July 2011, to make a video for their debut single caused more excitement, as did subsequent visits to radio and TV stations. By the time they played their first series of gigs in America – supporting Nickelodeon boy band Big Time Rush, in February 2012 – thousands of screaming fans were waiting for them at Chicago's O'Hare International Airport.

To an older generation, the commotion brought to mind an occurrence nearly 50 years earlier, when another group of fresh-faced, cheeky Brits had caused similar excitement. John, Paul, George and Ringo had come together to form what is still probably the most famous pop band of all time – the Beatles – and the phrase 'Beatlemania' was coined to describe the effect they had on teenage girls during their American tour. The screams at their concerts all but drowned out their vocals – much as they would later do with One Direction. But even the Beatles had not topped the US charts with their debut album.

As One Direction moved on through various capitals and countries, they were well aware of the role that social media was playing in their success and so made sure they found time to regularly post messages on Twitter, keeping fans updated on their lives. This way, even when they were far away, their followers felt closer to them and that they were sharing the experience. Their gigs involved a Q&A session midway through, which further strengthened the rapport and communication with their fans.

Things took a lot longer in the Beatles' day. They spent years honing their craft in Liverpool and, later, in seedy clubs in Germany's Reeperbahn. Social media consisted of newsletters and signed photographs sent out by their fan club. But the Beatles themselves had very little to do with this side of things.

The backing of Simon Cowell – an international brand in himself – has been of vital importance to One Direction's success. His fame, contacts, power and influence open doors around the world. Arranging a guest spot performing on the US or Italian versions of *The X Factor*, for instance, or introducing them to big-hitting music executives and record producers, is not a problem. 'Uncle Simon', as the boys nicknamed him, is always there for them.

It was Cowell's connections with the influential Nickelodeon TV channel in the US that first cemented their name in the minds of teenage America. A guest spot on the popular teen comedy TV series *iCarly* showed their fun side – as they effectively played themselves in a wacky storyline, ending with a performance of 'What Makes You Beautiful' – and won numerous prizes at the annual Nickelodeon Kids' Choice Awards.

They may be one band but they are very much five individuals in terms of personality, which is another important ingredient of their success. Don't like the mean and moody type? Try the polite and sensible one instead. Or perhaps the sexy flirt? The loveable joker? The excitable scamp? Just take your pick.

Such has been their storming success around the world that even broadsheet newspapers and the more cynical music publications have had to sit up and take notice – particularly after they sold out Madison Square Garden! They have also been honoured by waxwork models of them at the renowned Madame Tussauds in London – and don't forget those One Direction dolls that you can buy and take home to play with.

With a major world stadium tour planned for 2014, One Direction are intent on conquering countries they have never visited before, as well as returning to places where there will be even bigger, more hysterical crowds of fans waiting to scream at their concerts.

It's crazy, crazy, crazy. Welcome to the life of One Direction.

# 1

# Harry

The small village of Holmes Chapel in Cheshire has a history dating back to the 13th century.

It lies 20 miles north of Stoke-on-Trent and 25 miles south of Manchester. Having evolved as a traditional farming community, it is situated along and around the main route from London to Lancashire, which historically saw regular travellers stopping off at the various inns. Good rail and road links saw a rapid expansion in the population, which today stands at around 6,000. There are also several shops, a general medical practice, a church, a library and a secondary school.

The local pub, The Old Red Lion, dates back to the 17th century. In 1738, Church of England minister John Wesley, who founded the Methodist Church, stopped by at the inn on route from Oxford to Manchester to rest and to preach a sermon. In 1745, some of Bonnie Prince Charlie's troops took rest and refreshment at this same inn on their way from Scotland, in an attempt to reclaim the English throne for the Stuarts.

Two and a half centuries later, Holmes Chapel's most famous modern resident, Harry Styles, was still too young to drink there. This mop-haired former bakery boy was to make his mark throughout the world – not through religion or warfare, but with his record-breaking achievements in music.

He was actually born in Evesham, a market town in Worcestershire, on February 1, 1994, the second child of Des and Anne Styles and younger brother to Gemma, who was born on December 3, 1991. But shortly after his birth, the family moved to Holmes Chapel.

Harry Edward Styles' beamingly infectious smile has charmed female fans the world over and always delighted people from an early age. His mother has said that he had the natural ability to make people smile and, as a young child, loved being the centre of attention and making people laugh without any hint of shyness. Des always considered his son to be "a charmer".

At the age of two, Harry started attending a local nursery called Happy Days, which was run by a woman who occasionally babysat for him and Gemma when Des and Anne had a night out. He has fond memories of his time there and played happily with the other children.

This early integration with others helped him when he went on to Hermitage Primary School at the age of five. Mothers were allowed to spend the first morning with their kids in the reception class but, by lunchtime, Anne was pleased to be able to leave, knowing that her son had quickly settled. While some other children were crying and clinging to their mothers, Harry – dressed smartly in the school uniform of white polo shirt, grey trousers and navy sweatshirt – was having too much fun to care.

His best friend at primary school was a boy named Jonathan, and it was a friendship built to last. Despite his worldwide stardom, Harry has remained close to his true childhood friends and still sees Jonathan. They have kept in touch amidst his whirlwind life as one of the most famous and successful young singers in the world.

Back in his primary school days, Harry developed an early interest in maths that was more to do with being able to play with counting bricks than anything else. He later admitted that, as the maths got harder, he became keener on English and was very proud to receive an 'A' grade for his first essay. Unfortunately, he peaked rather too early and never achieved such a mark again; confessing to being easily distracted, although never terribly naughty, he was prone to chattering with his classmates and not paying enough attention to his teacher.

He was always something of a cheeky child, as well as a natural entertainer, and it was at school where he found an outlet for both his exuberance and his fondness for an appreciative audience. One of his first school plays was an updated version of the book and film *Chitty Chitty Bang Bang*. Harry, who loved *Toy Story*, had a bit part as that movie's miniature spaceman, Buzz Lightyear – reinvented as one of the toys in the store where the two principal children hide from the scary Child Catcher in *Chitty Chitty Bang Bang*.

He was to have his first starring role at the age of six, in that year's Christmas show, which made watching parents go all gooey-eyed. As well as the familiar nativity story, there was one about a mouse named Barney, who lived in a church. Wearing a pair of his sister's grey tights, a shapeless grey woollen jumper and mouse ears on a hair band, little Harry took centre stage as Barney. As the rest of the children sang a song about him, Harry – showing an early confidence in public performance – acted out the lyrics.

The parents loved it. It was ridiculously cute but Harry has always known how to play *cute*! He received a huge round of applause and didn't want to leave the stage.

Another memorable occasion for him was a family holiday to Disneyworld in Florida. His parents bought him a pair of droopy Goofy ears to wear, and he loved them so much that he took some persuading to take them off; the little natural performer would have worn them in bed if he had been allowed to.

It was his father, Des, who first inspired him to sing. Des, who worked in marketing and was 10 years older than Anne, was a big fan of two of the biggest acts in popular music history – Elvis Presley and the Beatles – and instilled in his son a lifelong adulation of both.

Des would play their records in the house over and over again, and taught Harry all the words to Elvis' 'The Girl Of My Best Friend'. When his grandfather, Brian, gave him a karaoke machine, Harry thought it the best gift in the world and was soon regularly singing along, mainly to Elvis songs. But he wasn't just into showbiz legends; he also went through a phase of being obsessed with the kids' band S Club Juniors.

Like many boys, Harry also liked playing with Lego. But whereas it's the building aspect that is the enjoyable part for most children, he was happy to let his sister, Gemma, do all the hard work in putting the pieces together to make something for him to play with. But then, Harry has always had a natural ability to win people over.

He discovered early in life that the power of personal charm would often get him what he wanted. As a school pal named William Rogers would tell the *Daily Star*, "Harry was always the charmer with the little cheeky grin on his face. He was always a really, really nice guy and got on well with everyone. He was very well liked."

At the age of six he was friends with a local girl named Phoebe Fox, who was the daughter of his mum's best friend. Showing an early flair for romance, he was determined to give her a teddy bear the same as his and pestered his mum to buy one for her.

"She was the cutest little girl," he later recalled.

Harry may have not been very creative with Lego, but he *was* experimental with food and displayed an artistic flair with his habit of painting a picture on bread with food colouring, then toasting it. His favourite sweets were M&Ms and he also had a passion for tins of mandarin oranges in syrup.

It was an idyllic childhood, at least for a time.

At home the boisterous boy showed an early predisposition to strip off his clothes on a whim for no particular reason – a habit that was to continue into adulthood! He would sometimes place his bed mattress halfway down the stairs and then leap naked from the top of the stairway to the bottom. The mattress would soften his landing should he not clear the stairs, but the nudity just seems to have been a part of his natural exhibitionist's streak!

Harry was happy at school with lots of friends of both sexes. More sporty than scholarly, his favourite lessons were PE and football, and he joined a local football team, Holmes Chapel Hurricanes.

"He wasn't the greatest footballer but he was really good with the girls," his former coach, Chris Rogers, would recall for *The Sun*. "Even at six, Harry was a charmer. He was timid and not the most physical on the pitch. Even at that stage I think he was protecting his looks. But he'd play anywhere to get a game. He scored a few nice goals from what I remember.

"He'd always have a quip and a smile with the guys – and with all the mums watching on the sidelines."

But at the age of seven, his cosy and contented little world would be shattered …

Unbeknownst to Harry and Gemma, Des and Anne's marriage had been crumbling over the last few years and they had eventually come to an agreement to split up. Once that decision had been made, the difficult part lay in telling their children.

Calling them into the living room, Des and Anne sat on the sofa with Gemma and Harry seated on the floor in front of them, breaking the shattering news as gently as they could. It was a traumatic time for everyone.

"Everybody was in tears," Des recalled for *The People*. In order to soften the blow, he said that he would not be leaving immediately. In fact, he carried on living in the house for another two years, sleeping in the spare room, before he eventually left for good.

"Of course I missed him [Harry] and Gemma," said Des. "When he was a baby I used to feed him every night, change his nappy and put him to bed."

Des remained in close contact with his children, seeing them every couple of weeks and supporting them financially. After their break-up, Anne reverted to her maiden name of Cox. She and her children moved from Holmes Chapel to a flat above a pub further into the Cheshire countryside where she became the landlady.

For a time Harry felt a bit lost, away from all the friends he had made in his old neighbourhood. But after a while he started hanging out with an older boy who lived nearby, named Reg, who was Gemma's age. They became good friends. Their biggest treat of the time was to ask their mums for some money and then cycle to Great Budworth Ice Cream Farm, about two miles away, to spend the money on good, real-dairy ice cream.

At the age of 11, Harry had his first kiss with a girl. Harry was at home with a friend and two girls, all watching a film on TV, when

Harry moved in for a smooch. "I think I pretended I'd kissed someone before because it was cooler," he told *Top Of The Pops* magazine.

When he was 12, the family moved back to Holmes Chapel and he started seeing a girl named Emilie, who became his first proper girlfriend. She was followed by Abi, who Harry describes as his first 'serious' girlfriend.

Whereas some boys of his age are awkward and shy around girls, Harry had always been as natural and at ease with them as he was with boys. Part of this was due to his natural confidence and good social skills, and partly because, after his father left, he grew up in a female-dominated household with his mother and sister. So Harry had many friends of both sexes, making him a very popular boy.

It was around this time that Anne also found love with a man named Robin Twist. She was relieved that her children also liked him, though she took things slowly with Robin and made sure not to have him in the house too much in the early phase of their relationship, for fear of upsetting Harry and Gemma. But it was Harry himself who encouraged Robin to come over when he started sending him text messages, asking him to visit.

Harry felt comfortable about having a man about the house once more. He and Robin got on extremely well, as they have continued to do to this day.

In the book *Dare To Dream: Life As One Direction*, Harry tells how he was delighted by Robin unexpectedly proposing to Anne on Christmas Eve, while the couple were watching *Coronation Street* on television: "I was at my girlfriend Abi's house at the time and I remember getting a call from my mum and how happy I was when she told me they were going to get married."

It took a while before they eventually tied the knot – another seven years, in fact. Harry, by then one of the most famous singers on the planet, would act as the best man, holding the wedding rings as Robin and Anne said their bows in front of 40 guests at Pecks restaurant near Congleton, Cheshire.

★   ★   ★

Harry fitted in well to his secondary school, Holmes Chapel Comprehensive, but he had grown a lot cheekier – never more apparent than when he dropped his trousers and underwear to 'moon'. It made the other kids laugh and getting a reaction like that only encouraged him. It was Gemma who was the more academic of the siblings, and he knew he would never be able to match her in that area.

Harry joined the local football team, the Wasps, with William Rogers, who played on Sunday mornings with Harry as goalkeeper. In 2008, he started a Saturday job at a local bakery, W. Mandeville – one of Holmes Chapel's longest established family businesses, situated along Macclesfield Road – where he earned £3.65 an hour. His work colleagues, aside from school pal Nick Clough who also had a Saturday job there, were older women who loved his cheeky ways and winning smile. They were also charmed by his habit of breaking into song when there were no customers around.

Harry would start the day with a big mug of tea and enjoy one of the bakery's favourite pastry meals at lunchtime – a brunch pasty packed with bacon, beans, sausage and cheese. Filling enough, one might have thought, but this was followed by the consumption of a vanilla custard slice or the rather grandly named 'millionaire's shortbread' which, in more humble terms, was simply a biscuit with caramel and chocolate.

As W. Mandeville owner Simon Wakefield recalled for the *Daily Mirror*: "He was really popular with the customers when he used to work on the counter. At night he would clean the floors. He was great to have around. There was always a good atmosphere when he was about."

Harry was also valuable in attracting female customers. "He was the most polite member of staff we've ever had. Customers really took a shine to him. The shop suddenly had an influx of girls when Harry worked here. Sometimes there would be 12 of them pouring in at one time. Even now, a group of 20 girls will sometimes come in and start taking photos of the shop."

In Year Eight at school, Harry became firm friends with Will Sweeny, whose mother is former *Blue Peter* presenter Yvette Fielding – then helming the *Most Haunted* paranormal investigations programme. The pair would regularly visit each other's houses after school. Both were outgoing, fun-loving characters who made each other laugh, sharing the same interests and sense of humour.

It was Will who was responsible for pushing Harry centre-stage as a singer in a rock band. Will had a drum kit and his friend Hayden Morris played lead guitar; the pair had begun jamming together three or four times a week after school and at weekends. Knowing that Harry was into music, Will suggested he learn bass guitar and join them, so he started looking on the internet for a suitable, affordable model.

But when they discovered that Nick Clough was already learning the bass, they roped him in and Will asked Harry be the lead singer instead. Harry showed unusual reticence, replying, "No, no. I can't sing."

But, after a lot of encouragement, he agreed to give it a go and started practising with the band. Often they would jam at Harry's house after school, in his bedroom decorated with a Manchester United shirt on the wall and some model cars. Even by boys' standards, it was very untidy.

"The first thing you would notice about Harry's bedroom was the mess. He was always getting shouted at by his mum because of it," Nick would tell the *Daily Mirror*. "Tidying up to Harry was just screwing things up and throwing them in the corners."

Nearby was a Chinese takeaway which the boys used a lot. A particular favourite to bring back to Harry's was deep fried crispy beef in Cantonese sauce. But Harry would think nothing of leaving the food cartons around afterwards.

Still, his bandmates were pleasantly surprised by his voice. "It needed work but so does everyone's, but you could tell he could sing," Will recalled. "He progressed really, really well although he was self-conscious about how his voice sounded. Every time he listened back to himself he'd be like, 'Ohh it sounds awful.'"

The budding musicians would stay at each other's houses at least three times a week and go out on a Friday and Saturday night. Although too young to legally drink alcohol, they did scrape together their pennies and persuade older lads to buy some beer for them at the shop. Saturday nights usually meant going into Manchester where the boys – who had various Saturday jobs – would spend their money.

When a new music teacher arrived at school, he initiated a Battle of the Bands competition in 2009 and the boys were one of 12 bands to participate. It wasn't until they were filling in the application form that they realised they had to come up with a name for themselves. Harry randomly suggested White Eskimo and, as no one offered anything better, they wrote that on the form.

Their most rehearsed and polished numbers were a fast-paced version of the Bryan Adams hit 'Summer Of 69' and 'Are You Gonna Be My Girl' by Jet, so these were the two songs that they sang. Dressed in their white school shirts and ties, they ripped into 'Summer Of 69'. Harry looked and sounded confident and the pupils responded well; he got them clapping along like a seasoned performer.

Bethany Lysycia, a fellow pupil who watched Harry at that performance, later told the local newspaper, the *Crewe Chronicle*, that everyone knew he had talent. He seemed to stand out from the rest and it was hard not to make him the centre of focus. "Everyone was really impressed, especially with Harry. We all knew he could sing because we would see him singing in the corridors all the time," she remembered.

Nigel Bielby, Deputy Head of Holmes Chapel Comprehensive, recalled, "Harry was always a performer. He was always a kind of social animal. As a performer, he would stand out from the crowd massively. He was always very, very charismatic, very charming."

White Eskimo were one of three acts to make it through to the final. An accomplished performance of their second number was enough to win them the competition and the £100 prize money. They also had four CDs of their tracks recorded at the school.

Harry's starring role with White Eskimo made him even more popular with girls at school and in the neighbourhood. He had always attracted female attention, but now he was being feted as the local celebrity.

"He had a lot of girlfriends through our school years," confirmed Nick Clough. "Whenever he had girlfriends he'd get them flowers and take them for meals. He used to cook candlelit dinners and give them gifts. He liked cooking."

Harry had only had eyes for one girl when he was 15: Felicity 'Fliss' Skinner. She lived in Solihull, West Midlands, over 70 miles from Harry, but she was introduced to him in the summer of 2009 while visiting a friend called Liv, who lived in Holmes Chapel.

"He was a really good boyfriend, very romantic and shy," Fliss would tell *The People*. "He was good looking and obviously I found him very attractive."

Harry was so smitten with Fliss that he even persuaded his mother to drive him and Will Sweeny to Birmingham to try to surprise her, knowing only that she lived in the Solihull area. "It was pouring with rain and it took hours to find her," Will recalled.

The sweethearts were together for just under a year before their romance fizzled out. "It was a long-distance relationship but it was a lot of fun. We just clicked straight away and got on really well," said Fliss. "He has a really cute smile. He was always singing to me when we were together. There was no real reason why we split up. We just drifted apart."

On Valentine's Day, 2010, he made a big romantic gesture towards a girl he had been dating but he was bitterly disappointed by her reaction. "I was going out with a girl who lived next to a park with a little stream running through it," he'd tell *Sugar* magazine. "So I bought loads of candles and laid them out along the bridge and when I'd finally lit them I called her and asked her to meet me. I'd been planning it all day, but she said she didn't want to come out. So I was just stood there, kicking candles into the stream and getting kind of upset. It was probably one of the most embarrassing moments of my life."

Another embarrassing moment was when Robin came into his bedroom and found him in bed with a girl. "She was down the side of the bed and my stepdad looks at her and out of nowhere I said to her, 'Did you find the remote?'" Harry told *Heat* magazine.

Meanwhile, White Eskimo continued to rehearse every Wednesday evening after school at Will's house – and then they landed their first gig …

★ ★ ★

In the spring of 2010, a girl at Harry's school approached him and said that her mother, who was getting married that June, wanted White

Eskimo to play at her wedding. The boys were surprised and flattered, but also worried when they were given the bride's playlist containing 25 numbers! But they diligently learned them all, significantly increasing their repertoire.

The bride loved them, as did another guest who happened to be a music producer. He told the boys at the end of the evening how good he thought they were, adding that Harry reminded him of a young Mick Jagger.

White Eskimo got paid £160 for the gig. It was their first professional performance and for the first time they felt like a real band. After this, they developed the confidence to start writing some of their own material.

But when Nick Clough suggested they create a more rock'n'roll image for themselves and get their ears pierced, Harry – who was always quite well-groomed – resisted, sheepishly admitting that he was worried what his mum would say!

In fact, when Gemma went off to university, the bond between Harry and his mother strengthened. "It was just the two of us. I went through a very hard time when his sister left for university – it was like I was going through empty nest syndrome," Anne would recall for *Teen Now* magazine. "I was alone in the house with Harry for a year so we got even closer.

"If I'd had a particularly bad day at work I'd come home to find he'd run me a bath and surrounded it with candles and even cooked me a meal. He just used to usher me out of the kitchen and say he'd got it all under control."

But he was still more than capable of being silly and mischievous on other occasions. One of his favourite games was to go to a supermarket with Will Sweeny and walk up and down the aisles, shouting and swearing at people, pretending he was suffering from Tourette's syndrome. They would also grab food and throw it over their heads to each other, attempting to catch it. Security staff were forced to guide them outside on several occasions; another game was to unexpectedly shout, 'Bogies!' as loud as possible to startle customers and staff.

"Harry loved it. He was always up for fun, wacky things, having a laugh, and he never cared what people thought," recalled Will.

Having finished his GCSE exams, Harry was planning to go to college to study law, sociology and business. But still, he remained rather clueless as to what he wanted to do in life. He knew he liked singing and loved being on stage and, like so many young people of his generation, he was a regular viewer of TV talent show *The X Factor*, which had become a phenomenal success since it began in 2004. Harry watched starry-eyed as young lads of his own age, such as Eoghan Quigg and Lloyd Daniels, showed that dreams can come true.

He often told his mother that he wanted to apply, but at other times he doubted whether he was good enough and so did nothing about it – until Anne took charge, filled in the application form for him and sent it off.

Harry was a little sheepish when he told his White Eskimo colleagues about *The X Factor*, brushing it aside by saying his mother had entered him for it and so he might as well go along. But to his surprise, they encouraged him. And Will Sweeny even went to the first audition with him ...

# 2

# Liam

Liam Payne was born on August 29, 1993. He was three weeks premature and his arrival caused instant alarm. It took a midwife several worrying moments before she was able to get a sound, or any sort of reaction, out of the newborn child.

This jittery start in life was to shadow him in his early years, when he would be in and out of hospital, having various tests done. Eventually, doctors discovered that one of his kidneys wasn't working and the other was operating at just nine per cent of its capacity.

Liam would need regular injections into his arm each morning to counteract this. The concern over his wellbeing led him to become very health conscious, both when growing up and as an adult. He would always avoid alcohol, was careful what he ate and kept very active.

Liam was the third child of Geoff and Karen Payne, who also had two daughters: Nicola, born in 1989, and Ruth, born in 1990. The family – including a dog named Della – lived in a suburb of Wolverhampton called Bushbury, in one of many modern redbrick homes on a residential housing estate. Geoff was an aeronautical fitter at Goodrich Aerospace and Karen a nursery nurse.

Liam shared his sister Ruth's love of music and dancing, and the pair drove their parents to distraction by their persistently loud singing on car journeys. As a toddler, Liam used to dance around the living-room to the theme tune of *Noddy,* much to the amusement of the rest of the family. He also loved *Toy Story* – and still does to this day. He pestered his mum and dad to buy him his own cowboy outfit so that he could dress just like the character Woody, and his most cherished possession was a Woody toy.

Like most young children, Liam had a vivid imagination. He viewed losing a tooth in a positive way because it meant a visit from the generous Tooth Fairy. He would write little notes to leave with his tooth at night under his pillow, and Karen would creep in with a written reply and some money in exchange. But his belief was punctured one such night when he saw his mum coming into his room, asking her, "What are you doing here?" However, as he didn't want to break the spell – or miss out on the money – he continued to play along with it for a few more years to come.

As the younger brother of two sisters, Liam was frequently seen as their plaything, who they often dressed up in girls' clothes! A girl named Harriet Thompson lived next door, and so Nicola and Ruth got together with Harriet's elder brother to 'marry' Liam and Harriet. They organised a wedding to which they invited both sets of bemused and amused parents. When Liam had to 'kiss the bride,' it was the first time he had ever kissed a girl.

As the children got older, Nicola, as the senior of the three, would often be left in charge of her younger siblings if mum and dad went out. Liam, meanwhile, attended Collingwood Infant School where, despite his sweet looks and gentle, polite nature, he would occasionally get into trouble for minor offences like water fights in the toilets, or climbing onto the roof to retrieve a football.

Early family holidays were usually spent visiting his grandfather, Ken, in Looe, Cornwall; Liam loved it when they visited holiday camps and he was allowed to sing karaoke. At the age of six, he was a big fan of Robbie Williams and sang his hit song 'Let Me Entertain You' in front of holidaymakers at a talent show. From then on he caught the performance bug, singing karaoke on almost every family holiday after that, even when they went abroad to Spain, Portugal or America.

Another singing idol was Oasis' lead singer, Liam Gallagher. An inventive little Liam would put his dad's sunglasses on, clasp his hands behind his back like Gallagher and sing along to his dad's Oasis CDs, pretending to be him.

An active boy, he joined successive scouting groups – Beavers, Cubs and Scouts – and threw himself into sports at school. He was disappointed at first not to be chosen for any of the school teams, but that was to change when he started secondary school at St Peter's Collegiate in Wolverhampton.

Liam tried out for the cross-country running team and startled everyone by beating the school's top runner to first place. Some of the pupils were *so* surprised that they said he must have cheated, but, the following week, they competed in the same race and Liam silenced his accusers by winning again. He had discovered his prowess as a runner and, showing a fierce determination later seen when auditioning for *The X Factor*, he focused on becoming as good a runner as he could possibly be.

He embarked upon an arduous training schedule that started with getting up at 6 a.m. every morning to go for five-mile runs before changing into his uniform for school. Returning home at the end of the day, he would pound a few more miles before his evening meal.

At the age of 12, Liam was recruited into his school's under-18s team, competing against others who were more men than boys, but he managed to keep up with them. He joined Wolverhampton & Bilston Athletics Club and became the third-best 1500 metres runner in his age group in the country.

He also enjoyed the school basketball team, and felt good wearing the superior quality basketball clothes bought on a family holiday to America. Unfortunately, some of the sixth-form boys thought he was too fond of himself and started to bully him. It was verbal rather than physical, but equally upsetting.

Liam eventually told his parents and teachers about it, but the bullying didn't stop and so more drastic action was required. His sister Nicola had a boyfriend named Martin who used to box, so Liam's parents suggested he go to the gym with him to learn how to defend himself.

In *Dare To Dream: Life As One Direction*, Liam recalled, "It wasn't the nicest gym in the world and you had to fight everyone regardless of age or size, so there I was, at 12 years old, fighting the 38-year-old trainer."

During his time in the boxing ring he had his nose broken, suffered a perforated eardrum and was always coming home with a bruised and puffy face. But, showing his familiar determination to triumph over adversity, he kept at it and even began to enjoy it.

At school the bullying continued, however, so Liam took another tack by asking a man he knew in his early twenties to pick him up from school, pretending to be his older brother. Then, one day soon after, the bullies chased Liam into the road after school and he decided to stop running, to face up to them. The boxing had given him confidence and he had a fight with one of them, which he won. He got into trouble with the head teacher, but he was never bullied again.

At the same time as his sporting prowess was increasing, so was his love of music. Nicola and Ruth had started to attend a local performing arts group on Sunday afternoons in the hall of Holy Trinity church in Sedgley, called Pink Productions. It had been set up by cabaret artist Jodie Richards in 2004, and aimed to get young people interested in performance.

An intrigued Liam went along to watch his sisters rehearsing one day and felt that this was something he wanted to get involved with. The group predominantly comprised girls, dressed in uniform pink tops – apart from four other lads who had been going for some time – and a shy Liam felt a bit out of place.

Jodie knew the Payne family, her father having worked with Liam's dad, and encouraged Liam to come out of his shell. But it wasn't easy.

"He didn't want to dance. All he wanted to do was sing," she recalled. "Normally they have to do both. But he needed his confidence built up and so the first show he did, called *Electric Dreams*, he just sang one song, 'Dancing On The Ceiling', and didn't get involved in any other part of the production. But during that show he got interested in the dancing and wanted to challenge himself and get involved."

But it was touch and go as to whether Liam's nerve would fail him at the last moment. "I literally had to push him on!" said Jodie. "He looked like a rabbit caught in the headlights. But by the second night he had the confidence."

It was evident to Jodie and to everyone who heard him that Liam had vocal talent. "His voice has improved massively over the years but he had a confidence about him when he was singing."

The other boys had all left by the time Liam did the first show in which he danced. "Liam has never been shy around girls," said Jodie. "So the fact that he was surrounded by girls didn't bother him at all. It just meant he got more female attention, and he didn't mind that!"

She remembers him being full of fun and very popular with everyone. "Liam and Ruth are particularly close and there was always a lot of banter between them. They used to cause havoc at rehearsals with their giggling. I would set a dance and Liam would end up on the wrong foot or Ruth would do something wrong and it was havoc. There were lots of laughs and jokes."

Liam played the main character of Tony Manero in a Pink Productions performance of *Saturday Night Fever*, dodgy lawyer Billy Flynn in *Chicago* and Prince Charming in *Cinderella*.

★   ★   ★

Alongside his creative and sporting flair, Liam showed that he also had a shrewd business head. One of his favourite TV programmes was *Dragons' Den*, in which budding entrepreneurs try to impress successful businesspeople with their ideas to gain financial backing.

Liam saw an easy way of making money in buying big boxes of sweets at a reduced rate and then selling them individually in the school playground, at a profit. He would make up to £50 a week doing this, which impressed his dad but was an activity he had to keep out of sight of the teachers.

It was Geoff who passed on his fondness for cooking to his son. The pair would often cook up a dish in the kitchen and Liam's speciality was a Chinese curry, using his dad's recipe. But oddly, Liam had developed a phobia of spoons as a young child, which remains with him to this day. He avoids soup because of this and, at breakfast, he would have cereal in one mug and milk in the other, so he could pop the cereal into his mouth with either his fingers or a fork, then take a sip of milk!

Ever keen to perform for an audience, Liam joined the school choir when he was 14 and cherished the moments when he got the chance to sing solo during a performance. Every lunchtime he would play football, and he regularly went to watch his local team, West Bromwich Albion. He even ran onto the pitch with other joyous fans when the team was promoted to the Premier League, in the 2007/8 season.

Meanwhile, on the running track he continued to shine, representing the West Midlands at 1500 metres. But during one school race, one boy showed spectators another side to Liam he would have preferred to have kept covered up!

"I was leading a race at school sports day when a lad pulled my shorts down," Liam would tell an Australian radio station, *Nova FM*. "Everything came out! It was all on show! That was a terrible moment for me."

Because of his sporting prowess and enthusiasm, his parents suggested that he might like to become a PE teacher. Liam was very taken with the idea – although he was also interested in becoming a fireman.

Things were going well on the romance side too. He became the envy of his friends at school when, aged 14, he started dating a girl in the sixth form, two years older than himself, who was also a friend of his sister Nicola.

"I thought it was really cool having an older girlfriend," he was to recall. But he was still quite naïve and a little too trusting of others. His friends took advantage of this by pretending that various girls liked him, so that he would make a fool of himself by making romantic approaches.

Having plucked up the courage to ask a girl out, only to be rejected, is a mortifying experience that chimes with many teenage boys. But there was one girl, named Emily, who Liam took such a shine to that he refused to take no for an answer. Showing his fierce determination, he asked her out 22 times. (We know this because he kept a tally!) Confident about his voice, he thought he might be able to serenade Emily and it did the trick – albeit briefly. She agreed to go out with him but dumped him the very next day.

Another girl he dated told him that she only wanted one of his hoodies for Valentine's Day, but Liam thought that "a bit rubbish" and instead boxed up the hoodie along with a teddy bear, 12 red roses and a Justin Bieber CD.

Meanwhile, his own love of singing gradually started to eclipse his enthusiasm for running – despite being on the 2007 reserve list, at age 14, for no less an event than the 1500 metres at the 2012 Olympics. He enjoyed watching *The X Factor* each Saturday night on TV and now felt ready to have a go himself. His parents were supportive, with Karen juggling her shifts at a nursery to accompany him for his auditions.

Liam had been undertaking work experience at Goodrich Aerospace where his dad worked, but had to take time off when the *X Factor* audition took place. In his first televised appearance, directly before his first audition, he told the TV interviewer in a strong West Midlands accent: "When I am school I think about singing all the time. I should really be concentrating on my work but I just think about singing too much. It's just a dream and I'd love to do it."

As he walked out before the judges – Simon Cowell, Louis Walsh and Cheryl Cole – wearing an open-necked white shirt, rolled-up sleeves, grey waistcoat and jeans, Louis asked him why he was there. A confident Liam replied: "I'm here to win. A lot of people have said I'm a good singer and that I've got the 'X Factor' but I don't really know what the 'X Factor' is and I believe that you guys do."

Liam then surprised everyone by saying that he was going to sing 'Fly Me To The Moon' by Frank Sinatra. But it was a song he knew well and had sung many times. He stepped quickly into it, without music, clicking his fingers to a beat like a veteran crooner. Simon did one of his trademark 'intrigued' inclinations of the head and Cheryl's face lit up. She beamed even wider when Liam chanced a cheeky wink at her!

Simon liked the performance but wasn't 100 per cent sure. "I think there is potential with you, Liam," he remarked. "I'm just missing a bit of grit, a bit of emotion and, actually, a bit of fun." He did have a point. Liam, although outwardly confident, did look rather too serious. He had shown he had the talent, but was his determination preventing him from relaxing and enjoying the moment?

Cheryl was charmed, however: "I like you. I think you are really cute. I think you've got charisma. You gave us that little cheeky wink." And Louis was the most effusive of all: "I think this kid could do fantastic in the show," he said.

Back to Simon: "You are a young guy; good looking. People will like you but there's something that I think is 20 per cent missing for me at the moment."

Liam promptly shot back: "Well, give me another audition and I'll show you I've got that 20 per cent."

The judges liked his reply and put him through to the Bootcamp round, where the remaining contestants received intensive coaching in singing, breath control, stage awareness and movement. Backstage, Karen hugged her son and declared herself "the proudest mum in the world".

Liam told *The X Factor Online*: "I've been singing since I was about six years old, doing karaoke. At the beginning of the [*X Factor*] audition I was quite nervous but as soon as I started singing I was all right."

At Bootcamp he joined in with the rest of the hopefuls, singing the Oasis number 'Stop Crying Your Heart Out' and Elton John's 'Your Song'. When he walked off, Simon turned to fellow judges Louis and Natalie Imbruglia, and said, "I like him." But there was a shock to come when Liam, along with some other hopefuls, was later told onstage by Simon that they would not be going any further in the competition.

Liam was devastated, mumbling backstage to host Dermot O'Leary that he felt something had been taken away from him. He had been confident and given it his all. But this time, his determination to succeed at whatever he put his mind to was not enough. He was going home... or so he thought.

Back onstage, there was unrest amongst the judges. Simon was shaking his head and then leant over to his colleagues to tell them, "I really think we are making a mistake here."

Louis replied, "I really liked him yesterday."

"I'm telling you, I think this kid has got a shot," seconded Simon.

Backstage, Liam was still coming to terms with no longer being in the competition when a member of the production team approached him to say that the judges wanted him back onstage.

He was startled and hadn't a clue what was going on, but he sensed that it was not all over. And he was right.

He returned to be told by Simon: "Liam, I don't often do this but it was such a close call with you. The other thing I want to say to you, Liam, is I think you've got something special. We've changed our mind."

An overwhelmed Liam bent over, held his head in his hands and sank to his knees. He was through to the last 24 acts – split four ways between 'Boys', 'Girls', 'Over 25s' and 'Groups'.

Later that day, on spin-off TV show *The Xtra Factor*, presenter Holly Willoughby asked the judges which of them had championed bringing Liam back. The others said it was Simon; as he explained: "It's a gut feeling. I thought we had made a mistake and on this show if you think you've made a mistake and have time to rectify it then you should do it."

The next stage was the judges' houses. Liam and the fellow singers in his category – Alan Turner, Austin Drage, Eoghan Quigg, Mali-Michael McCalla and Scott Bruton – were excited when told that they would be going to Barbados. But the six boys did not know who their judge was to be even when they were standing by the villa pool, until Simon walked out. They cheered loudly. Liam had got the judge he wanted. Simon was followed by former pop star (and his former girlfriend) Sinitta, who slinked her way next to him wearing a sexy gold swimsuit, making Simon look like a smooth and sinister James Bond villain.

The six contestants had fun playing on the beach together, re-enacting a *Baywatch* scene for the cameras and later chilling out by the poolside, only slightly marred by Liam getting sunburnt feet. But there was an underlying tension in the air, because only three of them would make it through to the live show finals.

First to perform, in front of Simon and Sinitta sitting at poolside, was 16-year-old Eoghan from Derry, Northern Ireland, who gave an assured rendition of the Cat Stevens song 'Father And Son'. Simon confided to Sinitta (and of course to the camera): "I love him, I think there's more to come from him."

21

Next up was Liam, the youngest boy in the competition, who launched into 'A Million Love Songs' by Take That. It was a composed and professional rendition. After he walked off, Sinitta said to Simon: "I love him. He has such a cute little face and a nice little voice as well." But Simon was less enthusiastic, commenting that his performance was only "good, not fantastic".

Mali-Michael, 15, from London sang the soulful Stevie Wonder number 'All In Love Is Fair', but Simon felt he went "off-key" at times. Essex boy Austin, 21, had stood out at Bootcamp and continued to impress with Michael Jackson's 'She's Out Of My Life'. "That last performance is going to change that boy's life!" Simon smiled when Austin had walked off.

Scott, 19, from Manchester, who gave up his job as a Bluecoat entertainer at Pontins holiday camp to follows his dream of stardom, sang Bonnie Raitt's 'I Can't Make You Love Me'. It was another strong performance by him, after which Simon told Sinitta: "That's what I like about him – he took on that song and really went for it."

Finally, Alan, 23, from Barnsley stepped up to sing 'All Or Nothing' by O-Town, which seemed to go down well.

When they all sang a second song, Liam put in a strong performance of 'Hero' by Enrique Iglesias. Then all the contestants had a nervous wait until the following day before hearing the verdict.

As they lined up before Simon and Sinitta, Simon told them that it had been a tough job picking his three finalists. "It was harder than I thought it would be but I've made all the right decisions for all the right reasons," he said, and then left a familiar dramatic pause to heighten the tension.

Turning his gaze on Scott, he told him: "I was disappointed in you yesterday – it was like listening to someone else. [Dramatic pause] But Scott... you made it!"

Then Simon told Eoghan: "You were so good throughout Bootcamp, and this is what I was looking forward to. But in my opinion you blew it. [Ridiculously long dramatic pause] "Even so... I'm going to take a chance on you."

Mali had told the camera beforehand: "I don't want to just go back to being an ordinary schoolboy. I don't want people to think of me as the guy who went on *The X Factor* and didn't do well. I want people to think of me as the person who made it."

But it was bad news when Simon told him: "There are moments, Mali, when you sang well, I thought you were brilliant. There were others you were so off-key it was like a different song."

Liam had told the camera: "I got thrown out once at Bootcamp. That feeling after you get thrown out was absolutely gutting. I don't want that again."

But once more, Simon told him that he wasn't going through. And this time, there would be no last-minute reprieve. "I'm a little bit concerned at the moment," he said. "On the plus side you look like the perfect pop star. But I've made a decision. It's bad news. The answer is no."

For Liam, Mali and Alan, it was the end of the road. As a despondent Liam slunk off, Karen, who had accompanied him to Barbados, gave her 'gutted' son a warm hug. She was later to recall, "I sobbed. He wanted it so much. He was devastated. But I knew he'd be famous one day."

Liam phoned Jodie Richards to tell her that he was out of the competition, and she collected him from the airport. Back in the UK, in an interview with Lorraine Kelly on *GMTV*, Liam said: "People don't realise how difficult it is to get to Bootcamp, let alone the judges' houses. Thousands entered and I was down to the last 24 and the last six boys. That was amazing."

He likened the competition to preparing for school exams, telling Lorraine that he would return one day. "I've done all the 'course work' and now I've got to go and pass the 'exam'."

Simon had told Liam to concentrate on his GCSE exams and to come back in two years' time – and so Liam set about doing just that. But it remained at the forefront of his mind, in fact he could think of little else during this whole 'waiting period'. It was almost like he was putting his life on hold until his chance came again.

Going back to normal life after the excitement of *The X Factor* was not easy. His TV appearances and interviews had made him quite famous, and his hometown community had got behind him to support his bid for glory. When he popped into his local McDonald's for a bite to eat, he was recognised and word spread so quickly that a large crowd of girls descended on him. A startled Liam had to call a security guard from the shopping centre to help him leave.

He also found it difficult to focus on his studies at school. "I had got a real taste for performing on a big stage and all I wanted to do from that moment on was to be a pop star," he later said, in *Dare To Dream: Life As One Direction*. "My schoolwork suffered quite a bit and my head of year warned me that my grades were slipping."

The pep talk worked and Liam eventually knuckled down to his studies, getting an A$\star$ in PE and two Bs, six Cs and a D in various other subjects. The school wanted him to stay on to sit his A-levels, but Liam was already focused in one direction. He decided to study music technology at the City of Wolverhampton College.

As determined as he was on returning to *The X Factor*, Liam had decided that if he failed to make it a second time, he would give up any notion of a singing career and instead join his dad at Goodrich Aerospace, as an apprentice... or perhaps become a fireman. *The X Factor* had become all to him and if he couldn't make it there, he didn't really want to make it anywhere.

Liam, who had now started dating local girl Shannon Murphy, went back to Pink Productions where Jodie's partner, singing coach Nigel Austin, continued to help him with his vocal training. As a local celebrity, he performed at various gigs and functions, which provided further good training. That Christmas, he was invited to perform at the annual switching-on of the festive lights in Wolverhampton city centre. Actor Paul Nicholas, who was starring in *Peter Pan* at the city's Grand Theatre, was the main attraction, and it was he who switched the lights on in front of hundreds of people. But still, Liam sang three songs.

The following summer, Liam stepped in for former Blue singer Lee Ryan, after he pulled out of the annual *Fun In The Sun* music festival at Rhyl in North Wales. Amongst other acts taking part were his *X Factor* colleague Alan Turner and eighties pop band Black Lace.

It wasn't a happy experience for him. His dad drove him to the gig on August 30, 2009, the day after his 16th birthday, but he wasn't very keen to go. It was a long journey and the fee of £50 didn't even cover the petrol money. When he got there, the notion of 'fun in the sun' was laughable. It was lashing with rain and he sang in front of a sparse crowd, before making the long journey back home.

A little while later, he was almost a knockout on a visit to his local skate park. Liam decided to try the biggest ramp there, but, as he whizzed downwards, his skateboard flipped up and he fell over, hitting his head on the floor and leaving a massive graze and bruises on his face. When he got home, Geoff told him that he had two new gigs lined up, which he had to perform in his bruised and battered state.

A far more pleasurable experience than the Rhyl gig was singing before 29,000 fans for a big match at Wolverhampton Wanderers' ground, when they played Manchester United in March 2010.

Yet all the while he was biding his time… waiting for his second chance of stardom.

# 3

# Louis

Cheeky, playful, loud – some people never change. Louis Tomlinson's One Direction colleagues see him as a big kid and he was just the same when he was a little one.

His mother, Johannah, once tweeted: "When Louis was a toddler he used to sit in his buggy waving to everyone, saying, 'Hiya! Have a good day!'"

Louis was born in Doncaster on Christmas Eve, 1991. His mother, Johannah – or Jay, as she is more commonly known – split from Louis' father, Troy Austin, when her son was two and Louis took the surname of his stepfather, Mark Tomlinson.

Louis' first word was 'cat', which his proud mum heard him say as he pointed at her parents' moggy in the garden. As an outgoing boy, confident and good-humoured, who liked to make people laugh, he was nicknamed 'Boo Bear' by his mother.

When she enrolled him into nursery, Louis took to it like a duck to water, eager to mix and play with the other children. Like many young boys of his generation, he was a big fan of the TV superhero characters *Power Rangers*, and usually asked for their tie-in toy versions for his birthday or at Christmas.

When he was four, the family moved to Poole, near Bournemouth, Dorset, on the South Coast of England. Louis has fond memories of his time here. Amongst the amusements along the seafront was his favourite Power Ranger ride, for which he was constantly badgering his mum for money.

Louis attended Uplands primary school and showed athletic prowess in the two years he was there, winning all of his races on sports day. He was well liked amongst the other pupils for his cheery and occasionally mischievous nature.

After two years in Poole, Jay fell pregnant with her second child, Charlotte, and the family headed back to Doncaster, settling in the village of Bessacarr. Louis was so overwhelmed by the arrival of a baby sister that he broke down in tears.

Now aged six, he was enrolled at Willow primary school and, in tune with his gregarious nature, soon made new friends. But his propensity to be the class clown frequently got him into trouble with teachers.

Mark Tomlinson worked at a lorry and van dealership in Sherwood, near Handsworth, and Jay was a midwife, so Louis was looked after by his great-grandparents, Edna and Len, until his parents came home from work. Louis was to form a lasting bond with them; Edna would pick him up from school and often take him to the park, while back home Len would make him ice cream.

Meanwhile, Jay and Mark had another daughter, Félicité, in 2000. Eight-year-old Louis, who loved young children, spent many happy hours keeping both his sisters entertained.

As a young lad his musical heroes were S Club 7, whose posters adorned his bedroom wall. Then, as he got older, he moved on to Busted – who were the first band that he saw play live. It was Busted's song 'Year 3000' that he sang after forming a band with some school pals for a Red Nose Day talent competition, aged 11, in which he 'played' a red inflatable guitar. He thoroughly enjoyed singing in front of an appreciative audience and it marked his first public performance. (Later, at around the age of 12 or 13, he became a big fan of Robbie Williams.)

When the time came for him to go to secondary school, Louis had to go to his and his family's second choice, Hall Cross. Here he made good friends with boys named Dan and Aiden, and it was through Dan that he met a girl named Arianna. She became his first proper girlfriend, who he dated for eight months.

But he never really settled at school, and so when a place became available at Hayfield, which had been his first choice, he left Hall Cross aged 13. Still, leaving all his old school friends behind was tough and it took him a little while to settle at Hayfield, as all the other children knew each other by that stage. But within a few weeks he'd started to make new friends and felt comfortable there.

During a school field trip to Norfolk, he shared a room with friends Geoff, Jona and Jamie, who were in a band called the Rogue with another boy called Stan (who later became Louis' best pal). One day Geoff casually mentioned to Louis that they were looking for a singer and suggested he have a go – despite not having heard him sing. Louis thought it sounded fun and so began practising with the band once a week. Their only public performances were when they played at end-of-terms for their school year group.

★   ★   ★

In 2004, Jay gave birth to twins, Daisy and Phoebe. For Louis, who has always been enchanted by children, they were the most marvellous additions to the family. He got on well with all his siblings, and living with so many females had the effect of making him at ease with women and girls – although he did still long for a brother.

As they were identical twins, Jay saw the opportunity to get Daisy and Phoebe involved in the acting business. She knew that more than one baby at a time was used for a single role during filming, so that one could rest and be fed while the other was on camera, and so the twins were much in demand by production companies. They appeared in the popular TV drama series *Fat Friends*, set around a slimming club in Leeds, West Yorkshire. When Louis – who had enjoyed acting in school productions – asked if he too could be an extra, Jay got the director to let him appear in the show. Louis would later say that he was one of the first people to ask James Corden – one of the stars – for his autograph.

Having caught the acting bug, Louis started going to drama classes in Barnsley and got himself an agent, who found him work in ITV1 drama *If I Had You* – about a police detective, played by Sarah Parish, who investigates the murder of a teacher. Louis made a brief appearance as one of a group of boys who finds the dead body. He also had a small part in the successful BBC1 school drama series *Waterloo Road*, and it was at this point that he decided he wanted to be an English or drama teacher, as it combined acting with the idea of working with children.

In year 10, when he was 14, he was fortunate enough to gain work experience at Barnsley Football Club because his grandfather knew the chairman. Louis helped out with the coaching, and enjoyed it so much that he decided he now wanted to be a full-time football coach.

In the meantime, he had a variety of Saturday jobs while at school, including sales assistant at Toys R Us and usher at the local Vue cinema, which was great fun because he got to see all the new movies for free. He also sold snacks at Doncaster Rovers' football stadium and worked as a waiter.

"I wasn't the best waiter, but I used to get good tips because I loved a chat, and maybe a little flirting here and there… " he would recall.

Louis passed eight of the 11 GCSEs he sat, failing business studies, history and geography. He was always flirtatious at school, but his attentions were later focussed on a girl named Beth who he went out with for a couple of years. But his propensity to have fun cost him dearly when he failed his first year of A-levels. Shock gave way to distress when he realised he wouldn't be able to re-sit them at Hayfield and that his best friends would be taking off to university the following year, leaving him behind.

So Louis went back to Hall Cross, to study for his A-levels all over again. He admitted to feeling "a bit of an idiot because I was a year older than everyone else," and he also had to make new friends once more. It was fortunate that he was so good at it.

It was during his sixth-form year at Hall Cross that he landed the lead role of Danny Zuko in a school production of *Grease*. He felt terribly proud to have got the plum part and gave it his all, being one of the highlights of his young life thus far. Unfortunately, 'his all' included the (unscripted and totally improvised) moment when he bared his bottom for a joke. It earned him a big laugh – and a week's suspension.

The show was also memorable for another reason. In the role of Frenchy, one of the 'Pink Ladies', was a girl named Hannah Walker and they began dating each other. (He had also developed a celebrity crush by now: on elfin actress Emma Watson, who played Hermione Granger in the *Harry Potter* films.)

That summer was a glorious one for Louis. He passed his driving test and was allowed to treat his grandmother's 1.2 Clio as if it were his own, as she hardly drove the car and was happy to let him make use of it. Louis revelled in the independence and excitement that comes with your first car and liked nothing better than driving himself and his friends to parties.

He and Stan – his pal from the Rogue – also went further afield, visiting France and Jersey. But it was when his parents went abroad on holiday for two weeks, with his sisters, that Louis saw the chance to have the party of a lifetime.

It wasn't that Jay and Mark were either naïve or unprepared. Suspicious of his keenness to remain behind and only too aware of his mischievous nature, they refused to let him stay home alone and insisted he stay with his grandparents. They wouldn't leave him keys to the house either, but Louis had a new key cut in advance and, once his parents had gone, wasted no time in inviting everyone he could think of to a party!

Stan brought along a powerful amplifier and, with the patio doors left open, it wasn't long before the police came knocking, telling them to turn the volume down. A worried Louis knew his parents would find out from the neighbours, so he thought it best to tell them the bad news while they were in good spirits. He put party photos up on Facebook, where he knew his parents would see them while they were on holiday. By the time they came home – and he had the house clean and tidy – the dust was settling and he got off quite lightly.

At age 18, one of Louis' favourite haunts was a bar called Priory, which had regular DJs and introduced him to all sorts of different music. He would eagerly look forward to going there at the weekend.

With music now more a part of his life than acting, Louis decided to apply to *The X Factor* in 2009. His audition was on a day he was supposed to be working at the cinema so he got a friend of his to cover his shift instead. (But when his friend forgot to turn up, Louis was promptly sacked!)

Jay drove him to the audition in Manchester and they sat outside in the queue for 10 long hours, in the freezing cold and pouring rain. But despite the adverse conditions and the lengthy wait, Jay enjoyed spending the time with her son.

"We were huddled together and chatting all day. It was time for just Louis and me. It was lovely," she later told the *Sugarscape* website.

Louis failed to get beyond the audition, but he knew that he wanted to try again. It had given him confidence and an extra determination to succeed, so it would prove an invaluable experience when he returned for another go the following year.

# 4

# Zayn

Growing up in a predominantly female household helped to shape Zayn Malik.

Born on January 12, 1993, in the village of Baildon, to the north of Bradford, West Yorkshire, he is the second child to Yaser and Patricia. His eldest sister, Doniya, is a year older than him and he has two younger sisters, Waliyha and Safaa.

It was a mixed race family. His mother, Patricia – or Tricia, as she is more usually called – has an Irish mother and English father, while English-born Yaser's father was from Pakistan.

The family later moved south of Bradford to East Bowling, and it was here that Zayn went to primary school at Lower Fields. He was a lively youngster, full of energy and a bit of a handful for Tricia. As a consequence of being the only boy amongst three sisters, he was also reserved and prone to feeling isolated, tending to shut himself away in his bedroom whenever he was unhappy, without sharing his concerns or anxieties with anyone else.

This led to him being comfortable in his own company as a young child; even today, he likes to get away and be on his own every now and then. But it has also served to make him something of a loner, who finds it hard to open up to others, doesn't make friends easily and too often retreats into his shell.

"I spent a lot of time on my own in my early years," he said in *Dare To Dream: Life As One Direction.* "I had my own bedroom so I would play with games and toys by myself. I was very independent and I still am in some ways."

He was a good reader at an early age and was encouraged to read a variety of books by his grandfather. This gave him a head start when he joined school but, socially, he took a while to fit in and settle. Being the only child of mixed race in his class made him feel even more of an outsider.

His former head teacher at Lower Fields, John Edwards, told the Bradford *Telegraph & Argus,* "I remember he was a nice young man, hard-working, and I remember in particular his leading role in the Year Six leavers' play."

Another issue that affected his confidence was his small stature. His first kiss, at age 10, took on a rather comical aspect when he had to get a brick to stand on to reach the girl's face!

Tricia had also instilled in him a superstitious streak. If anyone put an umbrella up in the house she would quickly tell them to put it back down at once; when a mirror broke, she took a sharp intake of breath and sombrely commented, "That's seven years' bad luck." Later, when Zayn began singing on *The X Factor,* he would brush his teeth "for luck" just before every performance.

As to the origins of his musical career, Tricia now recalls him singing a lot at home: "Zayn was always playing music on his computer and singing along to it for hours. I have quite a few videos of him singing as a little boy but he's banned me from showing anyone. My favourite is him singing 'I Believe I Can Fly' wearing a green dressing gown."

It wasn't until secondary school, at Tong High, that Zayn really began to develop confidence and to take an exceptionally keen interest in his appearance. (Years later, his One Direction bandmates would regularly rib him about looking in mirrors and grooming his hair.) Around the age of 12 or 13, he would get up half an hour before his sister Doniya in the morning, so that he could 'do his hair' before setting off for school.

Tong High had a much higher mix of races than Lower Fields, which made Zayn feel less conspicuous. Proficient at English, he took his GCSE in the subject a year early and got an 'A'; he was also good at art but not at maths, and, as his enthusiasm for drama increased, he was cast as one of the leather-clad 'greasers', the T-Birds, in a school performance of *Grease*. Aged 13, he featured alongside his friend Aquib Khan, who was later to star as a professional actor in the movie *West Is West*.

Zayn also appeared in a school production of *The Arabian Nights*, and played the title role in *Bugsy Malone*. He also joined the choir but, at that stage in his life, it was acting that gave him a real buzz, and he found confidence in immersing himself in characters. He decided that he wanted to be an actor or a drama teacher, and made up his mind to go to university to do an English degree.

In his drama class he formed a close friendship with a boy named Danny, who was a year or two older than him; together with Danny's younger brother, Anthony, the three of them regularly hung out together. But Zayn got into trouble too – most notably when he took a ball-bearing gun to school, and was given a stern lecture by the head teacher.

It was his music teacher who first suggested he try out for *The X Factor*. Zayn, who was then 15, got the application form but nerves got the better of him and he never filled it in.

That summer he had a growth spurt during the school holidays; when he returned to the sixth form, fellow pupils were startled by how much taller he had become. He had grown in confidence too, and suddenly girls were taking a keen interest in the handsome teenager with the moody looks. He even found his first real girlfriend, who he stayed with for nine months. But he still had plenty of self-doubt behind the cool façade.

With the next series of *The X Factor* approaching, Zayn got hold of another application form but, once more, failed to fill it in. The following year, he finally summoned up the courage to complete the form and send it off.

In the meantime, he had done well in his exams, passing 11 GCSEs. Deputy head Steve Gates remembered him as a "model student" and "star performer".

Now he hoped to show some of that star quality on stage in the biggest talent show around.

# 5

# Niall

Joe Dolan was a hugely popular singer from the showband era in Ireland, who also had a big international following. Born in 1939 in Mullingar, County Westmeath, he went on to have hits such as 'Make Me An Island' and 'Lady In Blue', and to build a firm and loyal fanbase.

His motto was, "There's no show like a Joe show." When he died, on December 26, 2007, at the age of 68, he was laid out in his coffin in his trademark white suit; thousands lined the streets of Mullingar to pay their respects to the town's greatest entertainer.

★ ★ ★

Niall Timothy Horan was born on September 13, 1993, in Mullingar, the second son to Bobby, a butcher for the supermarket chain Tesco, and his wife, Maura. The couple also had an elder son, Greg. The family lived on a street in the centre of the town, but moved to an estate on the outskirts when Niall was four years old.

Niall was a loving boy, and Bobby and Maura were both warm, caring parents, unreserved in showing love for their sons. When Niall first went to school, aged five, he hated being away from home and started crying as soon as Maura left him. But it wasn't long before his upbeat, lively nature kicked in; always game for a laugh, he soon made friends and became popular with the other children.

Their parents bought Niall and Greg two goldfish, which the boys called Tom and Jerry. Unfortunately, they died after the boys accidentally overfed them. With hindsight, it may seem like an omen of love that dies.

Bobby and Maura separated when Niall was six, after 15 years of marriage. For the next couple of years, Niall and Greg, who was six years older than him, divided their time between living at both of their parents' houses. They would settle at Maura's for a year, before eventually deciding to live with their father.

Bobby was delighted to take them in. Although the two boys were close to both parents, he had missed them and felt very lonely without his family around him. The boys preferred it there because Bobby lived in the centre of town, where they had friends and it was easier for them to get to school. But Maura remained very involved in their upbringing; they regularly stayed over at her house and she was a frequent visitor to Bobby's. Her relationship with her estranged husband remained good and he welcomed her considerable input.

But bringing up two lively boys as a working dad was not easy. The siblings would frequently argue and fight; during one particularly fiery incident, Niall split Greg's head open with a table-tennis bat! (Not so much 'love-all' as 'advantage Niall'.)

Amongst Niall's favourite playthings as a youngster were a tractor and a soldier's uniform. He also had a much-loved red costume to dress up as Po of the *Teletubbies*, as well as an imaginary friend called Michael who he would play football with.

It would only be after Greg left school and got a job – when Niall was 13 – that they started to get along. Being away from each other would draw them closer together.

In the meantime, Niall's first foray into music was playing the recorder at primary school. He would sing in the Christmas carol service and so impressed his singing teacher, Mrs Caulfield, that she suggested he try out for the town choir when he was eight. They too were impressed and he joined their ranks.

He also enjoyed football and performing in school shows, such as *Oliver!* when he was nine. The performer in him was emerging and he gained confidence under the spotlight. As Niall would recall: "I just always remember being really happy on stage."

At home and on car journeys, he always seemed to be singing. His musical idols were the Irish boy band Westlife – who he went to watch in concert – and Michael Bublé.

His aunt, who lived in America, would visit the family every summer to go on holiday with them to Galway, in the west of Ireland. They would also sometimes visit her in America. It was she who first predicted future stardom for the young lad, when she heard him singing a number by American country music artist Garth Brooks. She thought it was someone singing on the radio and was amazed to discover it was Niall. From then on, she often told him that he would be famous one day.

Around this time, an unusual occurrence was to leave him with a phobia of pigeons – after one flew through the open window of the bathroom while he was relieving himself.

Both Bobby and Maura were very aware of the psychological damage that a broken marriage might inflict on children, and they tried to do the best they could for their boys, maintaining good relationships throughout the family. It was Maura who taught Niall how to cook, and Bobby was impressed when his son showed an artistic flair with cupcakes.

"He had to look after himself a lot because I was working, so from the age of seven he had to do his own washing, his own ironing and often his own cooking," Bobby later told the *Sunday Mirror*. "To my mind all kids should be able to do what he can."

The boys did benefit by having two birthday parties each year – one with each parent. Bobby tried to be home by 4.30 p.m. on schooldays, but he had to start work early in the morning so Niall would have to get himself up to walk the mile-and-a-half to school. It was an upbringing that was to make him independent and instil in him some useful life skills. "He'll make someone a wonderful husband," a proud Bobby would joke to the *Sunday Mirror*.

Niall attended a rather strict Catholic boys' secondary school in Mullingar called Coláiste Mhuire. On his first day he bonded with a boy called Nicky during a geography lesson after Nicky loudly broke wind and Niall laughed loudly. Such was the foundation for both a firm friendship and the disapproval of their teachers.

The pair of them, along with another lad named Niall, would often sit at the back of class singing traditional Irish songs, which earned them a telling off from their teachers; another day, Niall bunked off from school and got into serious trouble.

It was this, combined with his general misbehaviour, that got him suspended for two days. And he was informed that he faced expulsion if his behaviour did not drastically improve. Being good at French and geography, but "rubbish" at maths, he generally couldn't wait to get out onto the playing field to participate in sports – particularly football.

The all-boys aspect of the Catholic school and the fact that he had no sisters, living in an all-male household, made girls – and any sort of romantic contact with them – something of a mystery to him. "I was always shy about that kind of thing," he said in *Dare To Dream: Life As One Direction*. "I had my first kiss when I was 11, but I think I've blocked it out of my head because it was so bad. I'm not sure it even counts as a kiss."

At the age of 12, he started to play the guitar; when he wasn't playing football, he liked to sit at home strumming and singing along. But he made so much noise that Bobby converted the garage for him, so he could play there and not disturb the neighbours. He was also into swing music, due to the influence of Bublé, so whenever he did karaoke he would get up and sing such numbers as Frank Sinatra's 'Fly Me To The Moon' – the same song Liam Payne would debut with on *The X Factor*.

As Niall's proud grandmother, Margaret Nolan, would tell the *Irish Independent*: "He was always a great singer. Even in the car, when his mum would put on a tape, he'd sing along. He knew when to come in with the music. He's a natural." He'd also taken to dyeing his naturally brown hair blond by this time – to better suit the image of a budding pop star!

When he was 13, he entered his school talent show – singing the Script's 'The Man Who Can't Be Moved', with his friend Kieron accompanying him on the guitar. The local newspaper took a picture and ran a complimentary article. This bolstered his confidence. After that, he entered a small local competition with Kieron where he sang 'With You' by Chris Brown. He was amazed to win.

When Boyzone singer Keith Duffy held his annual charity golf tournament in Mullingar, to raise money for an autism charity, Niall – who enjoyed playing golf – went along and asked if he could caddy for him. Keith agreed. He thought he was a nice, polite boy and gave him a tip afterwards; for his part, Niall was only too happy to walk around with a famous singer.

Niall also performed at the local *Stars In Your Eyes* talent show competition, organised by Gaelic football club Mullingar Shamrocks. Encouraged by the reception, he entered Ireland's big new 'search for a star' TV contest, *The All Ireland Talent Show*, on RTE in November 2009. He sang 'I'm Yours' by Jason Mraz, but he was not thought good enough to go beyond the preliminary stages.

Like the rest of the Mullingar inhabitants, Niall had grown up in the shadow of Joe Dolan. In the town's market square, a life-sized bronze statue of Mullingar's favourite son was unveiled in 2008. Despite his rejection at *The All Ireland Talent Show*, Niall wanted to follow in his footsteps.

Lack of confidence wasn't an issue – if anything, he was *overly* confident. When a local newspaper called him "Mullingar's answer to Justin Bieber", it did nothing to restrict his growing ego. But his good nature and winning smile won people over, and there was a child-like naivety about him which communicated warmth and charm.

His self-assurance was never more eminent than when he supported Welsh singer Lloyd Daniels – who had come came fifth in *The X Factor* in 2009 – at the Academy in Dublin, on April 6, 2010. Sitting on a stool and strumming his guitar, Niall sang Justin Bieber's 'Baby', 'Cry Me A River' by Justin Timberlake and 'Successful' by Drake.

One girl who was in the audience that night remembered him as being "a bit cocky" onstage: "It was like he was a professional singer and he had loads of confidence. His voice was OK but it wasn't that good and he was a bit full of himself. But he had the audience singing along."

Niall had his hair styled like Bieber and he was taking ever more care of the way he looked. He dressed smartly and was well groomed whenever he left the house.

He also had plans to go to university to study civil engineering, if he didn't make it as a performer. However, after watching Joe McElderry win *The X Factor* in 2009, a confident Niall went online to apply for the next series.

# 6

# *The X Factor*

## I

## HARRY

The day before he was due to audition for *The X Factor*, Harry Styles was physically sick. This was the first sign of the nervousness which was to recur later in the competition, threatening to ruin his chances.

He went to bed early that evening as there was to be a prompt start the following morning; when he got up at 3 a.m. he was relieved to find that the sickness had abated, although the butterflies in his tummy were still considerable.

He got dressed in a white T-shirt, casual grey trousers and cardigan with a scarf wrapped loosely around his neck. After quietly leaving the house in the dark, his family, plus Will Sweeny, got into their car and drove to the Trafford Centre in Manchester – all wearing specially made T-shirts with the words: 'We Think Harry Has The X Factor'.

When they arrived there was already a long queue of hopefuls snaked around the barriers, some of whom had been camping out overnight in tents. Various people were strumming guitars and singing; others chatted excitedly; some even managed to sleep! Joining the end of the queue, they waited for hours as the tension and nerves mounted with each shuffling step forward.

The audition process, staged at venues throughout the country, is long and tiring. Hours pass before the show's host, Dermot O'Leary, gets up on the small stage and greets everyone. Then the crowd is told to cheer and applaud and make 'X' signs with their arms, as the cameras film their movements. Dermot says his lines and they are repeated a few times before the crew is happy with the takes. Eventually, the crowd is let into the arena – where much the same thing happens again. This time, simulated 'handmade' posters are passed around for people to wave, bearing such slogans as 'I have the X Factor' and 'Pick Me Simon'.

By this stage, everyone is tired, cold and a little grumpy at being made to perform such 'spontaneous' actions. The excitement they felt early that morning is now a distant memory. Most just want to get it over and done with.

It's well into the afternoon before anyone actually gets to sing. They are called out in rows and file down towards the front of the stage to sing in front of producers in booths. Everyone can hear everyone else and it is a nerve-racking experience.

There is always much gossiping – and backbiting – going on amongst contestants, their families and friends. As one contender who went through the process at London's O$_2$ Arena remarked: "Some people with really good voices were dismissed and others who were appalling – and had people giggling – were waved through to the next round. It seemed that they were being put through just because they made for 'good television'."

Those who are given the thumbs-up receive a gold ticket to return a few days later for a second audition, at another venue. Only after that do the remaining contestants get to sing onstage. Making it to this stage means everything because all the hopefuls want to give it a shot in front of the celebrity judges; not only is it a step closer to their dreams, it also adds a touch of glamour and showbiz.

Thankfully, Harry passed through this early process and got his chance to sing before Simon Cowell, Louis Walsh and Nicole Scherzinger. All his family gave him good-luck kisses before he walked onto the stage.

Although he looked remarkably calm, he was later to admit to being incredibly nervous.

"I smiled and tried to look as confident as possible, but inside I was a right mess. This meant everything to me and I just wanted to do a brilliant job," he recalled in *One Direction: Forever Young*.

When Simon asked him to tell the judges something about himself, he replied, "I'm Harry Styles. I'm 16 and I work in a bakery on Saturdays. I've finished my GCSEs and I'm going to college in September." Simon enquired what he was going to study and Harry answered, "Law, sociology, business and something else, but I'm not sure yet."

Simon raised an eyebrow and remarked, "Wow. So what are you doing here today?"

"I've always wanted to audition but I've always been too young," replied Harry.

Simon nodded and Harry then launched into an *a cappella* version of 'Isn't She Lovely' by Stevie Wonder, finishing it with a little bow. The performance had gone down well with the crowd, who reacted with cheers and enthusiastic applause. To the side of the stage, Anne pumped the air in a victorious gesture. It was looking good.

Nicole seemed taken by Harry. "I'm really pleased we had the opportunity to hear you *a cappella* because we could really hear how great your voice is," she said. "For 16 years old you have a beautiful voice." Harry's family were smiling.

But then came Louis and to everyone's surprise, he put a dampener on things. "I agree with Nicole," he began positively, but added, "however, I think you're still young. I don't think you have enough experience or confidence yet."

After the boos from the audience had subsided, a clearly unimpressed Simon said, "Somebody in the audience just shouted 'rubbish' and I totally agree with them, because the show is designed to find someone – whether you're 15, 16, 17 – it doesn't matter. I think with a bit of vocal coaching you actually could be very good."

Harry seemed to be back on track. But was it enough? It was Louis who was first to make his decision. "Harry, for all the right reasons, I am going to say no," he said as boos filled the arena. Simon turned to

Louis and said, "I don't think they are booing you loud enough." Even Harry chanced a cheeky boo.

"I like you, Harry," said a twinkly-eyed Nicole. "I'm going to say yes." And Simon followed up with, "You'll be happy to hear that I'm going to be agreeing with Nicole. You're through to the next round."

As a delighted Harry walked off, Anne hugged him warmly. He had secured his place at Bootcamp. As Harry later told *The X Factor Australia*: "I remember being relieved when I got through because I didn't want to go back to school and say that I didn't get through.

"You've got through all this hard work and then you have to go home and tell everyone that you haven't got through. That was the main kind of brunt of it."

## II

## LIAM

Liam had waited for two years before trying out for *The X Factor* again – but it had seemed longer. He'd had a testing time with schoolwork, combined with various gigs, but nothing sustained its interest for him. All he wanted was another try and, in particular, to show Simon Cowell that he had improved.

He had worked hard at it, too. He had been taking vocal coaching lessons with Nigel Austin – the partner of Jodie Richards at Pink Productions – and felt that he was now mature and strong enough to be able to impress. He also chose a powerful song, designed to show off his voice to its best advantage – if he got it right! And if he didn't, it could all end in disaster. That was the gamble. Having heard Michael Bublé sing 'Cry Me A River' on TV, he'd decided it would be the ideal number for him and set out about rehearsing and rehearsing it until he felt he'd got it just right.

Back home in Wolverhampton, people had got behind Liam once more. Hairdresser Royston Blythe, who cut Liam's hair, decorated the front of his shop with banners hailing the local hero. Liam had sung for free at the salon's charity events.

"He's a very professional person," Royston told the *News Of The World*. "He's a very well-mannered young man and that's an added bonus because he's a great singer as well.

"Even from the age of 15 he had a great voice. When he came to the shop he was such a nice lad and, when we first heard him sing, we just knew he'd got it. We just knew he was going to get bigger and bigger. He was always a pin-up, even before he went on the show. All our juniors like him."

In Birmingham, when Liam walked onstage dressed in white V-neck T-shirt, jeans and boots, Simon treated him like an old friend. He waved to him and called, "Liam! How are you?"

Entering into the spirit of this casual approach, Liam smiled and replied, "Hello, Simon. Are you all right? I haven't seen you for a long time."

"Nice to see you," said Simon, and he looked like he meant it.

Backstage, Liam had told an interviewer from the show: "I know what it's like to be thrown out and I don't want to have that feeling again. I just want to get through. Simon said to me that I needed to go and get my GCSEs and that's what I've been doing. Today is my chance to prove to Simon that I have got what it takes. It will mean more than anything to get a 'yes' off Simon today."

But when he announced he was going to sing 'Cry Me A River', as made a hit by Michael Bublé, there was a hint of disappointment on Simon's face. Did he think it was too strong a choice? Had he heard it murdered too many times before? Or perhaps he just didn't like the song? Whatever the reason, Simon's face soon changed.

From the first long note, Liam held the audience in the palm of his hand and they immediately started to applaud. Guest judge Natalie Imbruglia smiled and soon people started getting to their feet. Simon half turned to look at the cheering crowd behind him, a slight smile playing across his lips.

Growing in confidence, Liam slowly walked along the stage, like a seasoned pro, while his mum, to the side of the stage, looked less confident, chewing her nails! At the end, with the crowd going wild, Simon stood up and applauded and was joined by Natalie.

It was a sight that Liam had not even dared to dream of for the last two years. And he couldn't stop beaming.

Cheryl Cole commented, "You've definitely got it. Whatever it is, you've got it. [She'd seemingly forgotten that *it* was the X Factor!] I thought your voice was really, really powerful."

Natalie added, "That was really impressive. I think that other people in this competition should be a little bit worried about you."

Louis too, was impressed. "Liam, I'm really glad that you came back," he said. "It was a brilliant, brilliant vocal. For 16 years it was so confident. You totally delivered." He then mocked Simon by saying to him in disbelief, "Simon, this is the guy you didn't put through."

But Simon refused to rise to the bait, telling him calmly, "He wasn't quite ready when he came to my house two years ago but I said to him then, 'Come back in two years' time and you're going to be a different person.' I got it right."

As Liam later reflected to *The X Factor Australia*: "You've got it in your head now that you want to go as far as possible. It's not just a bit of fun any more. So that's the most difficult stage to get knocked out, really."

With three 'yes' votes from the judges, Simon was the last to deliver. It was the moment that Liam had been waiting for, and it was unequivocal: "Based on talent... absolutely incredible," he said. "One massive, fat, almighty yes."

Liam clenched his fists and beamed from ear to ear. Later, he told an interviewer from the show: "I never expected in my wildest dreams to get that sort of reaction. My face hurts. I can't stop smiling. It was so amazing. Simon stood up for me and that was just the most amazing thing in the world, ever."

III

LOUIS

After having failed to pass the initial audition in 2009, Louis was determined to try again. He didn't tell too many people this time, just taking along his pal Stan for company. He had also taken a month of singing lessons, and his aim was to get to the judges' houses stage.

The pair drove down from Doncaster on the Friday night ahead of the Saturday audition, setting off at midnight and reaching Manchester at 2 a.m. Louis was amazed to see people already there, queuing.

Both boys were shattered, so Louis set his alarm and they grabbed a couple of hours' sleep in the car before joining the queue at 4 a.m. They took their sleeping bags with them and kept falling asleep so that people behind them would continually have to nudge them awake whenever it was time to move forward.

Louis' plan was that if he failed the initial audition, he would walk into a second one and hope not to be recognised! In the event, he passed at the first stage and joined other excited contestants in a holding room – for what seemed like an eternity – before it was time to go onstage. When he did, and he saw the celebrity judges and the audience for the first time, his mouth went dry.

Dressed in pale blue shirt, black tie, light grey cardigan and jeans, he started singing 'Elvis Ain't Dead' by Scouting For Girls, but was rattled when Simon stopped him and asked him to sing something else instead.

Fearing he had blown it and with a noticeable nervous quiver in his voice, he sang 'Hey There Delilah' by the Plain White T's. In truth, it was a shaky performance. Nerves had got the better of him and he breathed a sigh of relief when he was finished. As he would tell his mother, Jay, he wasn't pleased with the way it went.

Louis said afterwards that Nicole's smile all the way through his song made him feel better about himself. After all, she must have liked *something*. As for Simon, it was hard to fathom what was going through his mind.

Cowell took a no-nonsense approach, turning to Walsh to ask, "OK, Louis. Yes or no?" Although all the judges felt he was lacking in confidence, both Walsh and Nicole saw something in him and voted Louis through to the next round. "You've got three yeses," said Simon to a mightily relieved Louis.

Getting just two hours sleep may not have been the best game plan, but never mind. He had done it. He was through to the next round.

IV

NIALL

Niall stayed with his cousin in Dublin on the night before his audition, but was so excited that he didn't sleep. He got to the Dublin Convention Centre at 5 a.m. and was full of nerves.

"There were so many people there, I thought there was no way I was ever going to get through," he recalled in *One Direction: Forever Young*. His parents and brother Greg were with him, all huddled together to keep warm as they queued outside in the cold.

As Niall told an interviewer: "I want to be like one of the big names in the world, like Beyoncé, and Justin Bieber is a perfect example. I've been compared to him a few times and that's not a bad comparison. I want to sell out arenas and make an album and work with some of the best artists in the world. Today is the start of it. If I get through today then it's game on."

He was certainly 'game for it' by the time he got to sing before the celebrity judges. He wore blue jeans and a red-and-white checked shirt, striding confidently onto the stage to cheers. Smiling, he shouted into the microphone, "All right, Dublin!" like a headline act.

Katy Perry was the guest judge, and Niall joked with her about entering the competition. He said he was doing it so that he could be more popular with the girls at school – which was not strictly true, as he went to an all-boys school!

He sang Jason Mraz's 'I'm Yours', but was startled when Simon said it was a lazy choice. So then he sang his other song, 'So Sick' by Ne-Yo. When Niall was finished, Katy said, "I think you're adorable and you have charisma but I just think that maybe you should work on it. You're only 16. I started out when I was 15 and I didn't make it until I was 23."

Niall winced. It wasn't what he wanted to hear. He didn't want to be told to go away and try again when he was older.

Things were looking grim. A stern-faced Simon remarked, "I think you are unprepared. I think you came with the wrong song. You're not as good as you thought you were… [dramatic pause] but I still like you." Niall looked relieved and a cheer rang out from the crowd.

But once again, things took a downward turn. "You are obviously adorable," said Cheryl. "You've got a lot of charm for a 16-year-old but the song's too big for you."

Niall was on a rollercoaster ride, as Louis brought him back up with the words, "Niall, I think you've got something. I think people will absolutely like you because you're likeable."

It was Simon who gave him the first 'yes', and Niall punched the air with delight. But his jubilation quickly faded when Cheryl said, "No." An excitable Louis didn't wait for Katy and jumped in, saying that he was voting 'yes'. Niall needed one more 'yes' to get through. And it was all down to Katy…

"I agree with Cheryl," she said, to a worried Niall. "You do need more experience. And by the way, likeable-ness [that's 'likeable' in plain English] isn't going to sell records. It's talent, and you have a seed of it." But Katy finished as Louis Walsh had implored her: "Of course. You're in."

As a joyous Niall ran off, Simon muttered to Cheryl, "He's got something, Cheryl."

The X Factor, anyone?


# V

# ZAYN


On the day of *The X Factor* auditions, Zayn's nerves got the better of him once more – so much so that he refused to get out of bed! And there he would have stayed if it hadn't been for the intervention of his mum, Tricia, who persuaded him to get up and have a go.

"I was really nervous but she told me just to get on with it and not miss my chance," he recalled in the ITV documentary *One Direction: A Year In The Making*.

He eventually dragged himself out of bed at 3 a.m., feeling tired and sick with nerves, and drove down to Manchester, becoming increasingly nervous with every mile. Unlike many other hopefuls, Zayn lacked confidence and was plagued with doubt about whether he had any vocal talent whatsoever. Tricia had always told him he that he could sing, but – well, she was his mum, and mums say such things. What he really needed was a professional in the music industry to tell him that.

"I wanted a 'yes' from that audition. I just wanted somebody to tell me that I could sing," he said.

As Zayn was later to tell *The X Factor Australia*: "I didn't expect to get through as a solo artist. I didn't rate myself that highly."

There was a long wait to be heard but, in the end, the decision was a swift one. Having been given the green light to sing before the judges, a worried-looking Zayn stepped onstage. Taking a deep breath to calm himself, he nervously looked at Simon Cowell in front of him and, aware of his blunt attitude, wondered what he would say.

Zayn sang an *a cappella* version of 'Let Me Love You' by Mario, which he had been practising and which he felt suited his voice well. But he only got so far as a few lines before Simon raised his hand to stop him in familiar Roman emperor style. It was all over – for now.

Louis and Nicole put him through, and so too did Simon – eventually. But he added that he thought Zayn needed to be "hungrier" for it.

It was just the encouragement that Zayn needed to boost his confidence. He'd wanted to know if he could sing, and now he had three eminent figures in the music industry telling him that yes, he could indeed.

Harry, Niall, Louis, Zayn and Liam have a magical evening at the world premiere of *Harry Potter And The Deathly Hallows: Part One*, at the Odeon West End, Leicester Square, London, November 11, 2010.

Above and below: The boys travel in a luxury helicopter to promote their first single 'What Makes You Beautiful' in Glasgow, Manchester and London, September 11, 2011. DAVE HOGAN/GETTY IMAGES

Zayn hears the love at HMV Hammersmith Apollo, January 22, 2012. JO HALE/GETTY IMAGES

Liam is all smiles on NBC's *Today* at Rockefeller Plaza, New York, November 13, 2012. KEVIN MAZUR/WIREIMAGE

One Direction get a screaming ovation at the BBC Teen Awards at Wembley Arena, October 9, 2011. DAVE HOGAN/GETTY IMAGES

Niall strikes the right chord at Radio City Music Hall, New York, March 9, 2012. STEPHEN LOVEKIN/GETTY IMAGES

Harry is delighted to meet the fans at a CD signing for 'Up All Night' at Walmart in Somerdale, New Jersey, March 17, 2012.
BOBBY BANK/WIREIMAGE

The band arrives at the 2012 *Nickelodeon's Kids' Choice Awards* at the Galen Center in Los Angeles, March 31, 2012.

Zayn has that certain look at *Men In Black 3* New York Premiere at Ziegfeld Theatre in New York, May 23, 2012.

# 7

# Booted Together

In that July of 2010, all 211 acts left in the competition travelled to London, to be put up in hotels in preparation for the testing Bootcamp stage at Wembley Arena. Cheryl Cole was recovering from malaria, which she had contracted while on safari in Tanzania the previous month, and Dannii Minogue was on maternity leave. It left just two judges, Simon Cowell and Louis Walsh, on the first day.

Louis Tomlinson, who had always taken a carefree attitude towards life, was now experiencing just how tense, serious and nerve-racking it can be. And Louis Walsh turned up the heat by telling the contestants, "Bootcamp is tough. This is what it's all about. Showbusiness is tough. To survive in this business you've got to be tough."

Then Cowell fanned the flames further by telling them how Bootcamp could change their lives. As half of the contestants would be sent home at the end of the day, nerves were jangling as everyone was desperate to go on to the next round at the judges' houses.

The contestants were divided into four different categories – boys, girls, over-28s and groups – and given a song to sing. The boys had 'Man In The Mirror' by Michael Jackson; while Harry was happy with the choice of song, Zayn was not, worrying that he'd struggle with the high notes. In fact, Zayn was suffering a crisis of nerves that threatened to cripple his ambitions. When he heard some of the other boys singing, he was sure that he would be going home at the end of the day. Whenever there was a break in the proceedings, he thought he was about to be told to pack his bags.

"He looked very timid," remembers one of the production staff. "Whereas some of them had bravado and were noisy and would chat with all the others, Zayn often sat on his own. He looked like he would rather be anywhere else in the world!"

Zayn would be befriended by an altogether jollier and seemingly more confident boy. Like him, Louis Tomlinson knew that he did not have the strongest voice there, but he was determined to keep practising and give it his best shot. Liam and Niall also bonded when they shared a hotel room.

A total of 108 acts went through to the next day. There was a sense of relief when Simon told them that morning that they wouldn't be making any immediate cuts, and a buzz of excitement when, as a master manipulator of emotions, he told them he could already see a future star in every category.

For much of the day they would be having dance lessons given by creative director Brian Friedman. No one was more terrified of this than Zayn. He knew he couldn't dance and, being onstage with so many others from an all-round performing background, he felt frustrated and embarrassed.

When the boys were onstage, showing Simon and Louis the moves they had learned from Brian to the music of Lady Gaga's 'Telephone', eagle-eyed Simon suddenly stopped the proceedings. "Hang on. We're missing someone. Zayn's not there," he said. Friedman took the microphone to ask if anyone knew where he was, but nobody answered. Simon set off to find him and discovered him sitting on a chair backstage.

Zayn's disappearance hadn't gone unnoticed by the camera crew either, who had followed him. When the interviewer asked him why he wasn't with the others, he explained, "I seriously don't want to do it because I hate dancing. I've never done it before. I just feel like an idiot on stage with all the people who are clearly better than me. I'm not doing it."

But try telling that to Simon!

Zayn did just that when he approached Cowell, who, unsurprisingly, wasn't having it. "You can't just bottle it," he said. "You are ruining this for yourself. I'm trying to help you here. If you can't do it now then you are never going to be able to do it. Come on. Let's go do it."

Simon held out his hand and Zayn shook it. He followed him back to the stage, but was left with a stern warning not to duck out again.

Liam, on the other hand, thoroughly enjoyed the dancing. He had done it with Pink Productions and, although he knew there were far better dancers than him onstage, he saw it as fun and a relief from the pressure of singing.

Before they left for the day, they were all given a list of 40 songs from which they could choose one track to perform the following day. Oasis fan Niall chose 'Champagne Supernova', while Harry and Liam both chose another Oasis song, 'Stop Crying Your Heart Out'. Zayn and Louis also chose the same song, Bob Dylan's 'Make You Feel My Love', as covered by Adele.

On day three, there was a distinct heightening of tension as everyone had to sing before the judges in a televised performance, before receiving the verdict on whether or not they would be progressing to the judges' houses... or going home.

Harry's nervous sickness came back. He later admitted that when Simon told them all, "Today will be the most important day of your lives," he thought he was going to pass out!

As Nicole Scherzinger arrived to help the judges make the final selections, everyone clapped when she walked in. Harry was the first of the boys to audition, and it was an odd experience. He, like all the other contestants, did not receive any feedback from the judges and so had no idea how well he had done. It served to make everyone even more edgy. After he walked off to silence, Harry kept reliving the moment in his head, wondering if he could have done things better.

Even Liam – by now something of an old hand – was shaking before he went onstage. Just seconds before, he was still holding his lyrics to make sure he knew them off by heart. He had messed things up a little in rehearsals when he stumbled over the words and asked Brian

Friedman if he could start again. It did nothing to settle his nerves when Brian replied that asking to start again, when he performed before the judges, would be one of the worst things he could do.

Liam felt added pressure because his first *X Factor* audition in Birmingham, when he had sung 'Cry Me A River', had been so well received that now he felt too much was expected of him. Onstage he told the judges, "The reason why I think I've got the X Factor is because I had a knockback at an early age. I took on a huge challenge, I set myself a goal and I never gave up."

In the end, his rendition of 'Stop Crying Your Heart Out' was a polished and confident performance. He had chosen well. And when he left, Louis whispered to Simon, "Oh Simon, he's good." Nicole said that she liked him, but, somewhat surprisingly, Simon replied, "I like him but don't you think he's a little one-dimensional?" Louis disagreed, reminding Simon that Liam was only 16 and claiming, bizarrely, that he was "a young pub singer".

Everyone was pleased when it was announced that eight acts would be going through from each category, instead of six. But when all the boys were called onstage to hear the verdict, Louis, for one, thought that he wasn't good enough to progress.

One by one, they were announced by each of the judges in turn: John Wilding, Nicolò Festa, Paije Richardson, Aiden Grimshaw, Marlon McKenzie, Karl Brown, Matt Cardle. It was Simon who had the last say. "The final contestant who has made it through is…" he said, milking the drama and tension, "Tom Richards. That's it guys. I'm really, really sorry."

Liam looked close to tears. Niall held his head in his hands.

Backstage, Liam told the camera: "I just don't want to go home." Harry wiped tears from his eyes with a towel and said, "I'm really gutted." Niall was blubbing openly: "It's the worst feeling I've ever had in my life. Standing there, waiting for your name to be called and then it's not."

Liam was dreading having to tell his parents that he had not got through. He felt that he had failed them after they had given him so much support. But he eventually rang them and told them the news.

Louis was disappointed but not shocked. "I didn't even expect to get through the first audition if I'm being honest, so anything else was a bonus," he said candidly in *One Direction: Forever Young*.

Zayn said that he felt "crushed" at having come so far and having to return home. But Niall was already planning on coming back the following year.

But as the rejected acts started to leave and to try to come to terms with going back to normal life after so much excitement, the judges unexpectedly requested nine people from the boys and girls categories to return to the stage. A studio hand called out for Niall Horan, Louis Tomlinson, Zayn Malik, Liam Payne and Harry Styles, along with Sophia Wardman, Rebecca Creighton, Esther Campbell and Geneva Lane.

Niall and Harry were already outside the arena, sitting on the steps with their suitcases, ready to go home, when they were told to go back in. Niall had rung his dad, Bobby, to tell him the bad news.

As they walked back onstage, it was Nicole Scherzinger who explained: "Thank you so much for coming back. I know, judging from some of your faces, that this is really hard. We've thought long and hard about it. We've thought of each of you as individuals and we just feel that you are too talented to let go of. We think it would be a great idea to have two separate groups."

As this was starting to sink in, Simon clarified: "We've decided to put you both through to the judges' house." Cue mass screaming from both boys and girls – apart from Liam. For a few moments, he paused for thought. He had put so much time into being a solo singer that he didn't want to throw away all that effort. Quickly realising that to say 'no' would mean going home, however, he thanked his lucky stars that he was remaining in the competition and then got caught up in the jubilation, joining in with the mass hug.

Simon attempted to restore some calm. "Guys, girls," he said. "This is a lifeline. You have got to work 10, 12, 14 hours a day, every single day and take this opportunity. You've got a real shot here, guys."

They all knew it. They had come back from the brink in a way that none of them could ever have imagined. They were so excited that they wanted to get together and start practising right away.

Backstage, they all stood together in a circle. Harry remembers that their main preoccupation was what they were going to wear as a group. "How naïve we were," he later joked.

They had three weeks in which to turn themselves into a group before returning for the next stage, at the judges' house.

# 8

# One Direction

Harry, Liam, Niall, Louis and Zayn needed somewhere to practise. It was Harry's stepdad, Robin, who came to the rescue, offering the use of a bungalow in the garden at his house in Holmes Chapel. It proved to be the ideal environment, and it was here that they really started to bond.

"One minute we are solo artists and the next we have been put into a group with guys we don't really know and have to perform in front of people like Simon Cowell. It was massive pressure," Louis later told *The X Factor Australia*.

As Harry remarked: "We all had our own individuality and it was important that we kept that because that's what made us real."

Liam recalled: "I think the bungalow was the place where we really became a band. No one around us. No outside influences. Just us."

Living together 24 hours a day was a real test to see just how well – or otherwise – they got on. It was a time when they could find out about each other, their varying personalities, likes, dislikes and habits. There was a swimming pool which they used and plenty of room to play football. In the evenings they sat around a camp fire, chatting and jamming with Niall on the guitar. As the eldest of the group, Louis would drive them around. They would go for a drink and lunch at the local pub, or Harry would direct them to Great Budworth Ice Cream Farm, where they could sample a variety of flavours.

Inside the bungalow, they slept on blow-up mattresses or on the settee. After a long night of singing and chatting into the early hours, they promised themselves they would get up at 9 a.m. to rehearse, but it was more usually around mid-day – and then they would watch TV for a bit!

Favourite songs to rehearse were 'Crawl' by Curtis Brown, 'She's the One' by Robbie Williams and 'Fix You' by Coldplay. But, as Niall was later to admit, "We really didn't have a clue what we were doing."

Working out the vocal harmonies was tricky. At first, Liam tried to practise harmonising on his own but it wasn't working out, only coming together in a more natural way when they all started singing together. Gradually, they learned to play to everyone's strengths and a group began to truly form.

Harry recorded some of these early sessions. He still has the recordings but thinks they sound so rough that he has vowed that no one else will ever hear them!

"We got along well very quickly and we all fell into our little roles," Liam recalled later on Toronto TV channel *YTV*.

Harry expanded: "We went about it the right way. We just chilled out for a week. We made sure we were friends first."

More time was spent playing football and mucking around in the swimming pool than singing. It might have spelled disaster but, in fact, it worked in their favour as they all got to know each other.

Harry and Louis bonded quickly, sharing the same silly sense of humour. Zayn felt odd being away from home and living with this bunch of boys. Liam was the most focused and disciplined, while Niall was having the time of his life.

It was in this period that Harry came up with the name One Direction, as they were now all following the same direction as a group. When nobody else came up with anything better, they went along with it.

One night they were sitting round the fire, as usual, when they were startled by a cry from an adjoining field. Zayn went into the bungalow and got a stick to which he tied a rag and set it alight, to make a flaming torch. He and Liam led the way into the field but, in or after a brief moment, Liam was jumping back over the fence and hurtling towards them after being chased by a horse! All the others fell about laughing.

On another occasion, Niall was sitting on the toilet when Harry burst in and took a photograph of him. Sometime later, on Niall's birthday, Harry gave him a present – a heat-sensitive mug which displayed the picture of him on the toilet whenever hot water was poured into it!

After a week, they all headed home to see their families for a while and recharge their batteries, before preparing to head out to Spain…

★   ★   ★

The decision to form two groups, Belle Amie and One Direction, from soloists at the end of the Bootcamp stage was branded unfair by some of the other groups, as they had not originally been entered in that category. But Simon Cowell defended the decision to newspaper journalists.

"To be honest the groups who turned up weren't good enough," he said bluntly. "And anyway, the Wanted didn't suddenly walk into each other in a High Street. The same for the Spice Girls, Westlife, Jackson 5 – someone's got to be a catalyst. I thought it was fairer to put these singers in a group rather than let them go because they weren't quite there."

All eight acts in the groups category were booked into a hotel in Marbella, where they would be staying for a week. After settling in, they were taken to a luxury villa by the beach to discover which of the judges would be their mentor.

Zayn was left wide-eyed by the whole experience. Not only had he never been on a plane before, he had seldom come out of Bradford being entering *The X Factor*.

"Before *The X Factor* I had never seen a plane in real life," he said on the ITV documentary *One Direction: A Year In The Making*. "I didn't have a passport before One Direction. I never needed one. I wasn't planning on going anywhere."

He had been nervous before getting on the plane, and Louis made him feel even more jittery when, once they were in the air, he told Zayn, "This is where the plane does a loop the loop and goes upside down." Zayn actually believed him until Louis told him that he was joking.

Liam and Niall had a hunch that their mentor would be Simon, but the others were not sure. When Simon did in fact walk out, they all cheered and hugged him. He joked: "You had that dreaded thought it could have been Louis [Walsh], right?" Liam was especially pleased to see Simon because of the bond that he had already made with him.

As well as working hard, they got some time to mess around on the beach and to go out for a pizza. Spirits were high when they let their hair down back at the hotel. Niall's Spanish was good, which was useful in translating things for the others. The boys would shout at people out of the window and hide. Louis threw a pizza into the swimming pool and was surprised to get a good telling off – by Liam!

The song that the newly formed One Direction had chosen to sing before Simon and guest judge Sinitta was Natalie Imbruglia's 'Torn'. But panic set in after Louis got stung on the foot by a sea urchin. That night he slept through the pain, expecting it to be better in the morning. When he awoke, however, his foot had swollen to twice the size of the other one and was more painful than ever. When he tried to stand he fell over. Louis was taken to hospital, where he was given an antibiotic injection in his rear. It almost made him faint and he was sick afterwards.

Back at the villa, his One Direction colleagues were becoming increasingly worried because they were due to perform later that day and didn't know whether Louis would be back in time. If he wasn't then they would have to sing without him.

But Louis made it back and, although his foot was still a little painful, he managed to perform with the others in front of Simon and Sinitta, who were seated by the swimming pool.

The boys were also tense because two groups, Belle Amie and F.Y.D., had already been put through, with four others eliminated. Now it was just One Direction and fellow boy band Princes & Rogues, battling it out for the third and final place.

Liam and Harry took the main vocals, with the others backing and Zayn singing the last few notes in his soulful tones. It was a good performance; they had gelled together well, but the importance of the occasion – where just a 'yes' or a 'no' can change lives – made them a little tense and workmanlike.

Simon appeared to like what he was hearing but he wasn't giving much away. After they walked off, he looked at Sinitta and said, "They're cool, they're relevant. I think they were a little bit timid. I could see that they were nervous."

But that was for the cameras. Privately, he was knocked out by their performance, as he later revealed in an interview for *The X Factor Australia*: "They came out and I thought, 'Yeah. You really look like a proper group. Please, please, be good.' Within about 10 seconds I got goose bumps. I thought, 'They're not good. They're fantastic.' But I kept a very stony face."

When they returned to hear their fate it was delivered in classic Cowell style, veering from one position to another. As the five newfound friends stood in a line with their arms linked around each other's shoulders, Simon told them: "You are at a disadvantage because you haven't had the time that the other groups have had. On a more positive note – when it worked, it worked. My head is saying it's a risk and my heart is saying that you deserve a shot and that's why it's been difficult. So I've made a decision… Guys… I've gone with my heart. You're through."

The ecstatic boys whooped with delight and hugged each other, before hugging a smiling Simon. And then they jumped into the pool with their clothes on – apart from Louis, who had to protect his foot.

Later, as Simon sat by the pool, *Xtra Factor* host Konnie Huq pressed him to reveal his favourite member of One Direction. He replied: "There's normally somebody you have a connection with. It's very difficult to talk to five people all at once. You've got to talk to one person who gets it. I would say that you're kind of drawn to Harry's personality. He's very charming."

Simon would later tell *Rolling Stone* magazine that he recognised One Direction's huge potential as soon as they started singing in front of him.

And he confirmed that building as much drama as possible was integral – as cheesy as it was.

"I tried to keep a straight face for a bit of drama for the show. I remember sitting next to [Sinitta] who I was working with. The second they left we jumped out of our chairs and said, 'These guys are incredible!' They just had it. They had this confidence. They were fun. They worked out the arrangements themselves. They were like a gang of friends, and kind of fearless as well."

After flying home on a high, One Direction went back to their families and stayed in touch with each other by phoning and texting. A few days later, they would be on their way to London again for the live finals.

When they arrived in London they stayed in a hotel for a few days, as the house where all the remaining 12 acts from across the categories would be staying was not quite ready. When they finally moved in, they loved it. But not all the other acts shared their enthusiasm.

One Direction shared a bedroom which had white walls, white carpet and white bunk beds. It was pristine when they walked in but just moments later it was a mess! Not used to living away from their parents, they behaved like typical teenagers and their lively antics caused some friction and complaints.

Their bedroom carpet was obscured by a tangle of clothes all over the floor, with unmade beds and crumpled duvets adding to the disarray. Louis was singled out by the others as being the messiest of all. Niall and Zayn were always tidy back home so they didn't much like the mess themselves, but the small confines and lack of storage space made it difficult to be neat and orderly.

Louis was quickly established as the house joker, while Harry's habit of stripping off was fully exposed. Harry also kept the others awake at night with his snoring. One night, when he was asleep, the others drew a moustache on him with a marker pen to get their own back.

Niall was forever cleaning up after Louis, who would leave his clothes all over the floor. The room got into such a state that one day, when they were out, Esther from Belle Amie came in to clean and tidy it. But it didn't stay that way for long.

Zayn couldn't stand the mess. Back home he kept his room very tidy, and he didn't understand how the others could leave their belonging all over the place. He and Liam sometimes tried to clean the room, but gave it up because, as soon as Louis returned, it would be a mess within seconds. Louis, for his part, nicknamed Liam "Mr Tidy", joking that he was "the housewife of the group".

They lived mostly on takeaways after Harry tried to cook pizzas and almost burnt the house down. They were blackened and hard, but they ate them anyway.

There was a communal room where all the acts would meet and chat and unwind, with Wii games and table tennis available. But Konnie Huq was appalled when she paid a visit to the house.

"The One Direction boys are the worst," she said. "Harry put a banana skin in the bath. Their room is directly above the girls' [Belle Amie's] room and to wind them up they stamp on the floor when they're trying to get to sleep."

Harry stole one of the girls' bras and ran around the house with it on his head. Harry's pal from Holmes Chapel, Nick Clough, had bought him a gold snake-print thong for his birthday. He took it into the house and startled everyone by walking around in it – but caused even more of a stir by frequently walking around naked.

On another occasion, Niall was in the bath when Louis told him he needed something. Niall opened the door and a TV camera crew walked in!

The One Direction boys staged a further little prank when they bought Simon a card for his 51st birthday and taped £2.50 onto it – 50p from each of them. "You can buy whatever you want with it," Harry told him.

But it wasn't only One Direction causing havoc. Flamboyant Brazilian singer Wagner, the oldest of the finalists, regularly disturbed housemates' sleep by getting up at 5am to practise his martial arts. He would also sing very loudly. Irish singer Mary Byrne, another of the older contestants, complained of being kept up by the noise in the house.

There were regular clashes between Wagner and the One Direction boys, with Harry accusing him at one point of taking his clothes out of the communal washing machine and dumping them on the floor.

Despite complaining of a lack of sleep, Ms Byrne couldn't help but laugh at Louis's jokes and antics, while fellow singer Cher Lloyd also found him amusing. The boys also got on well with Aiden Grimshaw and Matt Cardle; on the first night in the house, they enjoyed singing along while Matt played the guitar.

Zayn, meanwhile, was continuing to find living with the boys challenging. He had grown up with sisters, and so all the noise and rowdiness was rather too much for him.

When One Direction heard that there was a picture of them in a newspaper, they were so excited that they all rushed out to the shop to buy it and then huddled around it. It was the first time that they had been in a newspaper as a band, so they rang their families to tell them about it.

The live shows took place at the Fountain Studios in Wembley, northwest London. The contestants' performances were televised on Saturday night, with a results show screening the following evening.

Louis' girlfriend from Doncaster, Hannah, was a regular visitor to the studios. Meanwhile, Harry – who everyone agreed was by far the biggest flirt in the group – had eyes for an older woman.

"Harry had a crush on one of the make-up artists," says a show employee who was regularly at both the studio and the house. "She was about 25 and he was incredibly flirtatious with her! She was amused by him but that was all."

Some newspapers had suggested that Harry was having a romance with Cher Lloyd, but in fact it was Zayn – who had also been linked with her at the time – who she really fancied.

"They both had a bit of a flirtation going and she liked to sit on his knee, which really wound up Belle Amie's Geneva Lane, who was a love rival – and a drama queen! But whether or not it went any further than a flirtation, I don't know. It was a hectic time with very little privacy, so I can't imagine they had the opportunity," says the source, who has asked to remain anonymous. Zayn also had a crush on fellow contestant Rebecca Ferguson, who was six years his senior.

Each of the Saturday shows had a theme. The first was number-one singles and One Direction sang Coldplay's 'Viva La Vida'. Earlier in the day, they had been given a makeover. Hair stylist Adam Reed said they had great hair to work with and he wanted to give them more of a modern feel. Niall's highlighted, light-brown hair made the most dramatic change when it was dyed what he described as "Eminem blond".

As their first live performance on TV approached, all of the boys were looking forward to it. They had practised hard to get their number right and were eager to show everyone what they could do – all except Zayn, who was once more in danger of being overcome by nerves.

When they had been practising the song with vocal coach Savan Kotecha, Zayn had been a little out of time and was now worried that he'd make the same mistake on the live show. But on the night it went well and they all got a real buzz out of it. Liam sang the opening lines, followed by Zayn and a smiling, confident Niall – the only one who looked like he didn't have a care in the world!

Louis Walsh was effusive, claiming the glory for having created the latest boy band – much to Simon's bemusement: "Guys, when I heard you were going to do Coldplay I thought it was a big, big risk but I loved what you did with the song. You totally made it your own. And I loved the way you have gelled. Even though Simon will claim he put this band together – it was my idea originally."

Simon gave him a withering look and replied, "It was *not* your idea." In fact, Nicole Scherzinger claimed to have first suggested it to Simon.

But motormouth Louis couldn't be stopped in full flow: "I think you have the potential to be the next big boy band but you have a lot of work to do. Simon, I'm not sure about the styling. Do you have a stylist?"

Simon's look verged on menacing, but he said nothing. Dannii Minogue tried to put an end to the bickering by saying, "Guys, I don't know whose idea it was because I wasn't there, but you look like you fit together, like you're the perfect band. That song was fantastic and you did make it your own. That was a perfect pop band performance."

Cheryl Cole also liked what she had seen and heard. "You look like you were meant to be together as a group," she said. "You've got all the ingredients for the perfect pop band. I reckon the girls will go crazy for you but you do need a little more time to develop as a group."

When it came to Simon's turn, he was clearly still seething from Louis' remarks. "Regarding your role in putting the group together, Louis, we'll rewind the tapes on that one. Essentially you guys came together because your Bootcamp auditions weren't good enough but you were too good to throw away. We took a risk and what was so impressive about that was – because it's a big leap going on this stage – when one of you started to screw up at the end [Louis Tomlinson appeared to be running out of breath], Liam stepped in and you brought it back together. That's what bands do. Regarding the style issue – I don't want to style this band because I want the band to do whatever they want to do. I'm not going to interfere. They can do it their way. It was brilliant, guys."

As Harry later recalled on *The X Factor Australia*: "The first live show was the most nerve-racking before we went out. But then it turned from us being really nervous to us just loving being on stage. Every time we were on we loved it and every time we came off we would be absolutely ecstatic from being on.

"For us to walk out and see all these girls... it was kind of scary, because obviously we had never experienced anything like that before."

It was Mary Byrne who received the most votes from the public in that first week, with Matt Cardle in second place. Cher Lloyd was third, just narrowly pipping One Direction. In a twist to this series, each judge was given a 'wild card' allowing them to bring back a rejected act from the judges' houses stage. This meant that the first two shows would feature double eliminations. Nicolò Festa and One Direction's fellow boy band, F.Y.D., would be going home.

The following week's theme was heroes, with One Direction singing Kelly Clarkson's 'My Life Would Suck Without You'. There was further drama for the boys during rehearsals when Harry started to feel sick again. The others knew that they would have to carry on without him if necessary, but, thankfully, he was well enough to perform that Saturday – although he was still feeling rough on the day.

In by now familiar fashion, Liam took the opening lines. But for this song it was Zayn who took secondary vocals, and the others joined in with the chorus. It was a rousing rendition which pleased the audience once again.

And once again, Louis took the opportunity to try to wind up Simon amidst his praise of the group. "Every schoolgirl in the country is going to love this song," he said. "My only problem, boys, is with your mentor. Simon... Kelly Clarkson, a hero?"

Dannii was also sure that the girls would love both the song and the boys. "You are five heartthrobs," she said, as they smiled back at her. "The true measure of a boy band like you is when you sing your big ballad. I will be looking forward to hearing that."

Cheryl was even more enraptured. "I can't even cope with how cute you are. Seriously. I just want to go over there and hug them. You are so sweet and adorable. I want to be saying, 'Wow! This is the new big boy band.' And I think that will come in time."

But Simon didn't think anyone had to wait any longer. "That time has just come," he insisted. "You are the most exciting pop band in the country today." Niall was so excited and delighted by this comment that he looked like he would burst. "There is something absolutely right," Simon added.

It was Matt Cardle who drew the most votes from the public that week – a trend that was to continue throughout the rest of the series. Mary Byrne slipped into second place and One Direction were third – although their percentage of votes was a long way down from the top two acts. Storm Lee and Diva Fever were eliminated.

The final 12 acts were given time out to go shopping in Oxford Street, central London, where they were mobbed by the crowd. They got to choose a free outfit in Topman and, that evening, Liam bought some cheap theatre tickets to see *Oliver!* When he got there, however, the manager recognised him and gave him complimentary expensive seats instead.

"The One Direction boys were amazed by the free things that kept receiving," says the show's anonymous employee. "They couldn't believe it when the wardrobe staff would give them bags full of clothes to take home. I think it boggled their minds that companies would want to give them stuff for free! It was very sweet how they didn't take anything for granted."

The finalists recorded a version of David Bowie's 'Heroes' to raise money for the charity Help for Heroes, which helps members of the British forces wounded in conflicts around the world. They also visited a rehabilitation centre at Headley Court in Surrey, where they met injured servicemen.

"The people here are real heroes," said Harry. "It makes you feel how lucky we are."

Meanwhile, Harry had won himself a prominent fan in the form of pretty 20-year-old actress Emily Atack, who played Charlotte Hinchcliffe in E4 comedy series *The Inbetweeners*. She cheekily tweeted, "Does Harry from One Direction HAVE to be 16?! Let's pretend he's 18 at least! Then there would only be One Direction he would be going… to the bedroom!'

Harry had another older fan in party girl Peaches Geldof, the 21-year-old daughter of Bob Geldof. She had asked to meet One Direction backstage after watching the Sunday night show and told them she was backing them to win. She cornered Harry and then told him that she needed his mobile number to text him to offer "spiritual guidance." Thinking this more than a little weird, he gave her a wrong number!

"I didn't want to give her my number," Harry told the *Daily Mirror*. "I don't need any spiritual help so I nodded along, and someone suggested I give her a fake number so I swapped around the last few digits."

Cheryl Cole had been looking forward to hearing a ballad from One Direction and, in week three, she got it. The theme was guilty pleasures. Simon had chosen their song for them but, during rehearsals, he felt that it didn't sound right and so they changed to Pink's 'Nobody Knows'.

It was a risk to change the song at such a late stage as they had to work doubly hard to learn the words and movements. With such a lack of practice, there was a definite concern that they might mess it up on the night. However, such fears were blown away by another solid performance.

"Guys, you just have to walk out on stage and everyone is screaming," said Louis Walsh. "It's like five Justin Biebers. Liam – a brilliant vocal from you. This band… you're really getting your act together. I think you *are* the next big pop band."

Louis had another dig at Simon later, when he told girl band Belle Amie: "Simon is putting all his energy into One Direction and it's not fair."

As Zayn later responded, "For Louis to say that was a bit harsh because it made us look like the bad guys."

Dannii also took a leaf out of Louis' book when she remarked, "Everybody wants to live your dream with you. Another great performance." Then, turning to Simon, she added, "I'm not sure why Pink is a guilty pleasure, though."

Cheryl got one of the biggest cheers of the night when she said, "You know what, guys? You *are* my guilty pleasure." Then, in one of the first allusions to Beatlemania, she added, "When you watch the VT [videotape] and see all the hysteria you caused when you went out there [shopping] this week, that's what boy bands should be about. Whenever the Beatles went anywhere they caused that level of hysteria."

For Beatles fan Harry, it was music to his ears.

Simon was full of admiration for their hard work and attitude: "The thing with you boys is that there are no bleating excuses – I can't do this, I can't do that. We changed the song and within 24 hours, practised and, I've got to tell you, apart from being a great performance, I thought vocally you have really made huge improvements. It is an absolute pleasure working with you lot."

Niall was very excited to get to meet one of his singing heroes, Michael Bublé, who was a guest singer on that week's show, and delighted to find how very down to earth and easygoing he was. Niall told Michael that he had bought tickets for his concert in Dublin but had to give them up because of *The X Factor*. Bublé replied, "Oh man. Any time you want tickets for one of my shows just let me know and I'll get them for you."

Solo artist John Adeleye was eliminated that week and One Direction came in third once more. They were to continue to be either third or fourth throughout the competition.

From early in the competition, the One Direction boys were clocking up large numbers of followers on Twitter and a firm and loyal fanbase was quickly building. At times, it seemed like when One Direction sang at the studios they were performing their own concert to screaming fans. And one particular member was attracting the most attention.

Every time Harry had a turn at solo vocals, the cheers and screams from the audience were decidedly louder. "Harry is getting loads of attention. It's the curly hair, that's where his power is," Liam joked.

"Harry was aware that he was the most popular but it didn't go to his head," said a show insider. "He wasn't arrogant or full of himself. He was confident but he had a nice way about him."

By now a real friendship had developed between the boys. They may have only known each other for a few weeks but their time together had been intense – from Robin's house to Marbella and now the *X Factor* finalists' house. They had got to know a hell of a lot about each other in such a short space of time.

Despite his anything-for-a-laugh antics, Louis frequently displayed a surprisingly disciplined side to his character. Whereas Liam seemed to be the natural leader of the group, with his more sensible disposition – the others called him 'Daddy' – Louis joined him in making sure that everyone got going and everything got done.

Harry was seen as the peacemaker who smoothed things over if ever there was an argument within the group. Zayn may have been regarded by the public as the quiet, shy one, but his bandmates insisted he was not like that around them. And Niall, as Liam said, "Just likes a laugh."

In week four, the finalists visited the London Dungeon tourist attraction, which brings together theatrical actors, waxwork models and special effects to recreate some of the scariest, darkest characters from history and folklore, including Jack the Ripper and Sweeney Todd.

It was in preparation for that week's theme of Halloween. The others laughed at Niall for being scared, but Liam, who had initial concerns about abandoning his aim of a solo career, now loved the camaraderie of a band and found going to the London Dungeon together, for example, much more fun that going on his own.

They also went to see Tinie Tempah at Koko in Camden, with Cher Lloyd and Mary Byrne. Tinie called them up onstage but Louis put his foot in it once again. He tripped on his way there and twisted his ankle. It hurt and he worried that it would affect that night's performance; in the end, he had it strapped up tight and took painkillers, and all was fine.

With claw marks painted red on their necks and more red make-up around their eyes, they sang Bonnie Tyler's 'Total Eclipse Of The Heart.' It was a gift to Louis Walsh, providing him with yet more ammunition with which to attack Simon.

"Everywhere I go I get asked about you. It's working," he said, before adding, "I'm not sure what the song had to do with Halloween."

Dannii wasn't interested in such quibbles. "You made vampires hot!" she said. And Cheryl didn't see them going home anytime soon. "I think you've got a really long way to go in this competition," she said.

Simon basically reiterated what he had said the previous week: "Once again, a great performance. What I really admire about you guys is – I know people are under pressure when they go into a competition like this, but you have to remember you are 16, 17 years old and the way that you conduct yourselves. You don't believe the hype, work hard, rehearse – it's a total pleasure working with you."

Belle Amie was eliminated. In an interview with the radio station *Viking FM*, band member Sophia Wardman commented, "I think it's a lot easier for the boys to do well because they're five cute boys and the girls are always going to love them and they are really good. I think for us, we just wanted a little bit more help, just because it's harder for us to get people to like us, to get the right song and the right styling.

"You could put the boys out there in bin bags and [they'd] sing 'Baa Baa Black Sheep' and they'd go through with flying colours. I think it's just a lot easier for them than us."

American anthems was the theme for week five, and One Direction sang a rousing version of Kim Wilde's 'Kids In America'. One Direction was Simon's last remaining act in the contest, but he was confident that this week they would really make their mark and "stamp out the opposition". With a team of cheerleaders behind them, it was their most enjoyable song so far. But would Louis be pernickety about the song fitting the theme? Of course he would!

"A brilliant way to end the show," he shouted over the cheering audience. "The hysteria is growing on this band and you remind me a little bit of Westlife, Take That, Boyzone. I love everything about the band… but Simon, I'm going to have to get my rule book out. The theme is 'American anthems'. This was not even a hit in America. It was sung by Kim Wilde who is from London. It's not an American anthem." Looking directly at One Direction, he declared, "Your mentor has cheated."

Dannii was less excitable than Louis – but then of course, most people are. "It was a great performance guys. I don't think, vocally, it was the best of the night, but a great performance," she said.

Cheryl – whose crush on them was showing no sign of abating – commented, "That absolutely cheered me up. It made my night. I thoroughly enjoyed it. I love chatting to you backstage. You are just good lads. A great performance. Good song choice." Then, glancing at Simon, she added, "but it isn't American."

But Simon was determined not to let anyone rain on his or One Direction's parade. "When you came out it was like sunshine on a beautiful day and then Louis [Walsh], the thundercloud, comes along and drizzles on everything that is happy." Turning once more to One Direction, he added, "That was your best performance by a mile."

Meanwhile, female solo singer Treyc Cohen was eliminated.

★　★　★

After their performance, One Direction popped outside the studios to wave to their fans. Cheeky Louis wore a hospital gown and when he turned round, the back part was tucked into his star-patterned boxer shorts!

An invitation to the premiere of the latest Harry Potter movie, *Harry Potter & The Deathly Hallows*, was a treat for the finalists – in particular Louis, who still had a crush on pretty actress Emma Watson, who played Hermione Granger.

The One Direction boys had a surprise in store; they were seated in a room, all dressed and waiting to go out, when the star of the movie, Daniel Radcliffe, walked in. They were amazed when he said, "It's quite weird and thrilling to be meeting you all because I have been watching you every week."

Louis couldn't resist asking him, "How fit is Hermione?" Daniel looked a little embarrassed but replied, "Very. But she is also like a sister to me."

When they turned up at the cinema, the crowd lining the red carpet were calling the band's name. The boys were still getting their heads around being celebrities.

Ms Watson greeted them all with a kiss – something Louis could only have dreamed about a few years earlier. She looked stunning in a black lace dress and short Peter Pan hairstyle. But during the screening of the film, Niall fell asleep, much to the others' embarrassment, and they had to nudge him to wake him up.

They were also invited to the annual Pride of Britain Awards, which recognises unsung heroes. Dressed smartly in suits, they and their fellow guests marvelled at tales of unselfish heroics which were awe inspiring and often tear jerking.

Backstage, former England footballer turned presenter Gary Lineker jokingly told Liam off for flirting with his attractive wife, Danielle. Simon Cowell, who knew Danielle, had invited her along to *The X Factor* a couple of weeks before, after she told him she was a huge fan of the show. He also introduced her to the judges and contestants backstage. Liam had, rather awkwardly, told her she was beautiful. To his embarrassment, she'd obviously also told her husband because Gary approached him and said, "I need to have a word with you about flirting with my wife." He was joking and Liam knew it – but then Danielle came over and kissed Liam on the cheek, saying, "This is my new boyfriend!"

Back onstage, that week's theme was songs by Elton John. It sounded pretty definite, with little room for artistic interpretation. Simon chose 'Something About The Way You Look Tonight' as the boys' song.

Their performance was polished and they showed a true unity, born of a growing confidence each successive week. Louis – no doubt to his irritation – could find nothing with which to niggle Simon. "After that performance I think you are only going in one direction and that direction is the final," he said.

"You are so consistent. It's scary. That was great," said Dannii.

Cheryl echoed Louis, "You definitely are heading in one direction."

Simon took the opportunity to publicly praise how pleasant they were behind the scenes: "Guys, I want to say something. This is the first time, in all the years of *X Factor*, where I genuinely believe a group is going to win this competition. That was so impressive. You've seen all the girls and everything else but you've remained focussed, you've been really nice to the crew. You're nice to the fans… most importantly, everything that happened tonight, from the choice of song, to what they wore, it was all down to you. Guys, congratulations."

As if to demonstrate their niceness, the boys were upset when Aiden Grimshaw, who they had become good friends with in the contestants' house, was eliminated.

Earlier that following week, they went to watch an international football game: England v France. Afterwards they met several of the England team, including defender Rio Ferdinand. They were taken aback when Steven Gerrard said that his wife and kids were massive fans of One Direction.

The theme for week seven was songs by the Beatles. One Direction chose 'All You Need Is Love' and Harry was very excited, having grown up to be a big fan of the Beatles, as was Liam. As the weeks went by, vocal coach Savan Kotecha was adding more and more complicated harmonies into their performances. The boys knew they had to step up and continue to improve and impress.

Wearing similar suits (or in Harry's case, the same one) to those they wore at the Pride of Britain Awards, the song perfectly fitted them. It was fun both for them and for the audience.

When it came to the judges' comments, they could barely be heard above the continual cheering. "A lovely arrangement of the song," shouted Louis. "It's good to see the fab five singing the fab four. You've lifted your game. I think you are in for the long haul."

There were more rousing cheers, but Dannii wiped the smiles off the boys' faces after a promising opening remark. "Another fantastic performance," she said. "I've always given you good comments. I just have to say tonight, you guys were struggling with the backing vocals."

As boos rang out, Cheryl said, "That was another great performance from you guys." A slightly peeved Simon added, "As ever, you worked hard and delivered a fantastic new version of the song."

On the live results show the following day, all *The X Factor* contestants sang the Help for Heroes song, 'Heroes'. It went straight to number one. Paije Richardson was eliminated from the show and now only seven acts were left: One Direction, Matt Cardle, Mary Byrne, Rebecca Ferguson, Wagner, Cher Lloyd and Katie Waissel.

Louis had paid a visit home to Doncaster shortly after the previous show and bought a standard class ticket on the train – but after sitting down he was mobbed by fans demanding autographs, which he happily signed. Rail staff were so concerned about the situation that they moved him to first class – where he still had to sign another 10 autographs!

It was a welcome break from the mad world he had entered and a chance to relax with his family, who were pleased to see him too. He also welcomed a good night's sleep in his own bed.

Jay told Sheffield's *Star* newspaper: "Louis thought it was great. They have to fend for themselves more down there [in London] than he does at home. Here he gets a cup of tea in bed!"

After travelling back to London, One Direction visited the HMV shop with the other finalists to help promote 'Heroes'. In week eight, each act got to sing two songs. The theme was a flexible one – rock – and Harry was influential in choosing a song he first sang at his school's Battle of the Bands competition a year earlier, with White Eskimo: Bryan Adams' 'Summer Of 69'.

It was a high-energy performance that had everyone on their feet. Midway through they walked off the stage and around the back of the judges to be nearer the audience, encouraging the crowd to clap along.

Once more Louis Walsh, as the first to respond, found himself having to shout over the cheers. This time he had no quibbles about their choice. "I loved the choice of song," he said. "The competition would not be the same without One Direction."

A smiling Dannii remarked, "You've really stepped it up. I liked that." Cheryl also felt they had raised their game. "There's electricity in the room. It's fantastic. You are growing and growing and getting better and better."

Simon was keen to prove that he was a much more 'hands off' mentor than people assumed: "I'd just like to say that I had nothing to do with this song choice. Harry chose the song. It was a great choice."

Having already met one of his singing idols, Michael Bublé, Niall was delighted with the guest singer that week: Justin Bieber. He tried to play it cool by going up to him and saying 'hello', but as he walked away, Liam spotted the danger signs and quickly escorted the starstruck Niall out of the studio. He could scream with excitement outside!

Their second song was Joe Cocker's ballad 'You Are So Beautiful'. Louis Walsh was bristling from the opening bars. It was a stripped-down version to show how far they had come vocally and they all took a turn at solos – apart from Louis Tomlinson.

"You proved tonight you are not just a boy band. You are a brilliant vocal group," said Louis. "I loved everything about it but... the only thing about it [looking at Simon], I don't think it's a rock song, Simon. I don't really think it's in the rules."

While Simon raised his eyebrows, Danni commented, "There's only one word for that and it's stunning."

"It's great that you have fun and dance and all of that but I absolutely loved watching you just standing there and singing," said Cheryl. "I think you've got a really bright future as a boy band."

Simon light-heartedly put Louis down. "If I could just deal with Captain Boring's little comment about it not being a rock song," he began. "Joe Cocker actually was a rocker, Louis. Do your homework. Go and buy a book or something." Louis took it well – he even laughed. "Guys, this was, in some ways, my favourite. Zayn in particular: you have grown in confidence."

Two acts were eliminated, Wagner and Katie Waissel. The end was nearing for everyone as the semi-final approached.

That week One Direction went to another film premiere, this time for *The Chronicles Of Narnia*. Dressed in black suits with skinny ties, they resembled the Beatles more than ever. It began to snow outside as they walked down the red carpet in London's Leicester Square, complementing the magical qualities of the film.

The boys also went bowling that week, and each of the remaining acts had to film a video for what would become the winners' single. But it was a difficult week for One Direction, because Zayn had to take time off to return home to Bradford after the death of his grandfather. They had been very close, and Zayn remembered him as always joking and smiling. His grandfather had been ill for some time and had suffered several strokes. He had watched One Direction singing 'You Are So Beautiful' on the show, and it became his favourite song. He had said that he wanted their version of it played at his funeral – and so it was. Liam, Harry, Niall and Louis all went to the funeral to show their support.

That week Harry fell ill. After complaining of feeling drowsy, he had to see a doctor, and their mentor, Simon Cowell, was also absent due to illness. Things seemed to be falling apart for them at a crucial stage in the competition.

While Zayn was still in Bradford, the others rehearsed without him. The theme for the first song was club classics, and they had chosen Rihanna's 'Only Girl (In The World)'. The second song had no theme. Simon had asked all the remaining acts to choose something that they thought would get them to the final. One Direction chose the haunting 'Chasing Cars' by Snow Patrol.

After Zayn had returned, they all woke extra early on the Saturday morning (at 8 a.m.) and were rehearsing at the studio 30 minutes later. 'Only Girl' was a great choice for them because they could really belt it out and get the crowd behind them.

"You deserve to be in the final. You've got something special," said Louis. Dannii too liked them more and more. "I really want to see you next week. That was brilliant," she said.

By now they were used to glowing remarks, so they were a little taken aback by Cheryl's slightly diffused reaction. "That song for me was a little bit dangerous only because it's so current right now," she began. "It's Rihanna's record and you have to make it like it was your own and not written for her… and I don't know if it quite worked for me. But I hope to see you in the final."

Simon was quick to jump in, saying, "I thought the song was absolutely perfect for you. That's what I liked about it. They didn't take a safe option. They had the guts to do it."

'Chasing Cars' beautifully showed off Harry's harmonising skills. "You've definitely got something special. I think you are the next big boy band – but I said that last week," said Louis. He had actually said it *every* week!

"Boys, you have got through such a tough week and that was a classy performance," said Dannii. "You've grown up in front of our eyes. We've never had such a good band on *The X Factor*."

Cheryl spoke for most people in the show when she acknowledged, "All the crew, all the staff, everybody has become so fond of you guys over the past few weeks. This week I was so impressed. You didn't have Zayn, and Simon wasn't around. You showed a real level of maturity. You really deserve a place in the final."

Simon, seemingly with little more to add, said simply "That was a great performance."

"They were so pleased to be there that they were very good natured," agrees one of the backstage staff. "One of the things that really struck me about them was how compliant they were. Simon Cowell's right-hand man, Tim Byrne, was very hands on with them. So even if Simon wasn't around, it wasn't as if they weren't being organised. And things like haircuts and hairstyles for the live shows were very much a decision by Syco (Cowell's production company) committee.

"This was the case with most acts in the show but more so with One Direction. More time was spent with them. Harry's hair would be a meeting in itself!"

Another employee of the show who worked closely with Syco confirmed that the boys were well liked for their easygoing, polite nature. "The guys were really popular backstage – definitely my favourite *X Factor* performers," he said.

Mary Byrne was eliminated by the semi-final results, which left four acts to battle it out in the final: One Direction, Matt Cardle, Rebecca Ferguson and Cher Lloyd. In the days leading up to it, the boys all got to visit each other's hometowns and to see their families. It was a clever stroke by Cowell, not only making the boys feel happy but also drumming up as much support as possible.

Unfortunately, snow meant that they were unable to get to Ireland, so the boys spoke by live video-link to Niall's family there. At Louis' school in Doncaster, Hall Cross, they were given a rousing reception from screaming fans who held homemade posters proclaiming their support for him and the rest of the band.

"I was really overwhelmed," Louis later told an interviewer from *The X Factor*. "I thought there would be some support but not as much as that."

Inside the school hall, they were introduced by the Mayor of Doncaster, Peter Davies, as they waited backstage to perform. As the audience chanted, "One Direction!", Louis confided to the others that he was more nervous than on a Saturday night at *The X Factor*.

They walked on to piercing screams and Louis told them, "Thank you very much everyone for coming. I really appreciate your support." They sang the first song they ever performed together, 'Torn', and went on to sing 'Chasing Cars' and 'Summer Of 69'. It marked the first time the group had performed to an audience outside of *The X Factor*.

Mayor Davies said he was delighted to meet Louis and would be watching the final on Saturday, adding, "Thousands applied to *The X Factor* and to make it to the final is an amazing achievement. It is wonderful to see talent like this coming from Doncaster. I hope that as many people as possible will vote for Louis and the band. They are excellent ambassadors for the town."

Then it was on to Harry's hometown of Holmes Chapel. The village had been adorned with banners, balloons and signs proclaiming, "Welcome Home Harry". A sizeable crowd had gathered outside the family home and as they approached in their blacked-out car, deafening screams of "Harry! Harry!" rang out from local children, as well as fans who had travelled there from further away. Teachers at the nearby Hermitage primary school had allowed pupils to take time out of lessons in order to be there.

Emerging from the car, Harry, Liam, Louis, Niall and Zayn signed autographs for fans before heading inside, where they enjoyed champagne and cake with Anne, Robin and other family members and friends. Robin told Harry how great it was to have him back, along with the rest of the boys. "You're all family now," he said. A tearful Anne told him, "You'll always be my baby, no matter how big and famous you become."

Most of the shops in the village carried messages of support in their windows. The W Mandeville bakery, where Harry had a Saturday morning job, had a loaf of bread in the window with the words, "Vote 1 Direction & Harry". Harry took his bandmates there to show them around, chat to the staff and tuck into some brunch pasties. He loved the window display, and inside, a range of cakes with the words 'X Factor' and 'One Direction' iced onto them were proving a big hit with customers. Harry's mum, Anne, had bought some of them and took them to the *X Factor* studios to give to the boys, and also to Simon Cowell and presenter Dermot O'Leary.

Next stop was the HMV shop in Zayn's home town of Bradford, where they gave a signing session for the fans. Zayn's headmaster at Tong High, Steve Curran, told the local *Telegraph & Argus*, "We're all behind [Zayn], it's been mentioned in all our assemblies."

Zayn couldn't get his head around being just a rather quiet, anonymous boy when he left Bradford a few weeks earlier and returning as a star, with girls chasing after him and screaming his name wherever he went. He told the others that he had never gone out of his way to attract attention and that, only a month ago, he'd been no one. And now this!

They had never seen a bigger or more excitable crowd than the one that converged on HMV. "It's weird going into a shop where I normally buy my CDs from and [to] have that reaction," said Zayn. "I'd love to go in there one day and see our single on the shelf."

That evening, they travelled to Liam's home town of Wolverhampton for a gig. Simon joined them there and everyone was chanting their names as they appeared at Queen Square, with police holding the crowd back. The band sang 'Viva La Vida', 'Only Girl (In The World)' and 'Chasing Cars', before it ended with fireworks.

Nearly 4,000 turned out to watch them perform in the freezing cold. The gig gave them a taste of what life could be outside of *The X Factor*, and made them even more determined to stick together no matter what happened in the final.

But the occasion was slightly marred when 35 people had to be treated for minor injuries. Some had to be lifted over barriers after a surge from the crowd. The medics said the injuries were mostly caused by the cold and overexcitement; several girls had been waiting too long in the cold with insufficient clothing, while others had felt faint due to lack of food and hyperventilation.

Niall's 80-year-old grandmother, Margaret, flew in from her home in Westmeath with Niall's parents, Bobby and Maura, and their son Greg, to watch him in the final. She had been a huge fan of *The X Factor* ever since she watched the first show in 2004, while recovering from a hip operation. But she'd never dreamed her grandson would be on it one day.

Niall was later to credit the show for bringing his parents closer together. They both regularly turned up at the studios to support him and talked a lot more to each other than they'd normally have done. Bobby also got to know and like Maura's new husband, Chris.

Meanwhile, Liam had split with his girlfriend, Shannon Murphy, and started quietly dating a 22-year-old backing dancer on the show named Danielle Peazer. There was to be no theme for the final, which was stretched across two days. One Direction chose Elton John's 'Your Song', and the second number on that first day would see the finalists singing a duet with a celebrity. The boys were overjoyed when they heard that they had Robbie Williams, who was a personal idol of Liam and Louis.

After they had sung 'Your Song', Louis Walsh said, "It's amazing how five guys have gelled together so well. I know you are all best friends. I've never seen a band cause so much hysteria so early in their career. You have an amazing future."

Dannii praised their commitment: "Guys, you have worked so hard in this competition. You are so together. You deserve to be here and I'd love to see you in the final tomorrow."

Cheryl, too, didn't want to see the last of the band that always put a smile on her face. "I have thoroughly enjoyed watching you guys growing every week, having the most amount of fun possible and I think you deserve to be standing on that stage tomorrow night."

Series favourite Matt Cardle had earlier sung Dido's 'Here With Me', which was full of emotion and was one of his best performances of the series. Rebecca Ferguson's version of Corinne Bailey Rae's 'Like A Star' was also moving and powerful. With two extremely strong singers in the final, Simon was getting worried about his boys.

As he admitted: "After hearing the first two performances tonight – Matt and Rebecca – they were so good that my heart was sinking. And then you came up on stage and... you are only 16 and 17 years old... and each of you proved that you should have been there as individual singers."

Perhaps he was forgetting that it was his decision to put them into a group? But Simon thought Robbie Williams would be the ideal performer for them to duet with. Not only did they admire him, but years earlier he had first forged a career for himself in another boy band: Take That. Simon also liked the choice of song, Robbie's hit 'She's The One'.

All of the boys were very excited. Liam told *The X Factor* interviewer, "This is the one person who I really wanted to sing with."

"He's inspirational," added Liam.

"I think it's incredible that he would even consider doing a duet with us," said Harry.

Liam sang the opening, as usual, but surprisingly his voice faltered when he attempted the top note in the line, "and *if* there's somebody..." He winced slightly but carried on.

When Robbie Williams – never short of confidence – swaggered on to join them, Niall looked fit to burst. Robbie looked like he was enjoying it as much as anyone, putting his arms around their shoulders one moment and high-fiving them the next.

Simon was loving it, too. He sat with the other judges with a big smile on his face, nodding along to the music. Afterwards, Robbie urged viewers to vote for One Direction.

Louis loved the harmony and announced: "We've got five new pop stars."

Dannii had no doubt that – win or lose – they were going to stick around: "That was a fantastic performance. Whatever happens tonight I'm sure you guys are going to go on and release records."

Cheryl agreed: "I really think that you have a massive future."

Simon simply commented: "I would love to hear your names called out at the end of the competition because I think you deserve it."

Some of the biggest names in the music industry had been brought in to duet with the finalists. Rihanna sang 'Unfaithful' with Matt Cardle; Christina Aguilera sang 'Beautiful' with Rebecca Ferguson and Will.i.am sang 'Where Is The Love?/I Gotta Feeling' with Cher Lloyd.

But at the end of the evening it was Cher who was eliminated. The following day – the very last of that year's competition – One Direction came full circle by choosing to sing 'Torn', which they first performed in front of Simon and Sinitta in Marbella as a newly formed band. Matt Cardle sang Katy Perry's 'Firework' and Rebecca Ferguson covered Eurythmics' 'Sweet Dreams (Are Made of This)'.

"We wanted to win so much," Harry was later to tell *The X Factor Australia*. The boys had given it their all in one of the toughest finals in the show's history. When they were voted into third place, behind runner-up Rebecca and the winner Matt Cardle, they were naturally disappointed.

But no one thought that One Direction wouldn't continue. They had seen the adulation around the country. They had performed at gigs to rapturous crowds; they knew they were getting better and better. What was more, they liked each other and wanted the dream to continue.

'Torn' was both their first and last song in the show, but now it was time to perform outside of *The X Factor*. Simon put his arms around them onstage and announced, "All I can say is this is just the beginning for these boys."

Niall, for one, was in good spirits and optimistic about the future. When his brother Greg asked him how he was feeling, he smiled and said, "On top of the world," adding that he "couldn't have asked for a better year". Zayn too was upbeat and positive. As he told Dermot O'Leary: "We are definitely going to stay together. This isn't the last of One Direction."

# 9

# All Directions

Just before the winner was announced for *The X Factor* 2010, Simon Cowell whispered backstage to One Direction that, if they won, he would take them for a holiday to Barbados. When they came third, Liam turned to Simon and quipped, "No chance of that holiday then?"

They all laughed, and it certainly helped to lighten the moment. Despite being determined to carry on, they were experiencing a feeling of deflation that their *X Factor* dream had ended after so much hard work. Harry took it particularly badly and had to be consoled by his mum, Anne. Zayn went off on his own for some quiet time.

Niall took it well but it was Liam who was the most composed and level-headed. He felt sure that the future was going to be good for them, but he had to do a press interview on his own because the others didn't feel emotionally up for it. Liam did manage to rally them to do one for *The Xtra Factor*.

After the show's final, they went back to the contestants' house to spend their final evening. The next day, Simon called them into his office at Sony to discuss their future. Even though he was no longer in front of the cameras, he was still giving it his *X Factor* shtick.

"I've made a decision," he said. After a long, dramatic pause, he told them that he was going to sign them to his record company.

It was the perfect antidote to what they'd all been through. The one piece of news they had been hoping for: the all-important record deal. The boys let out a huge cheer and hugged everyone – including Simon.

"This was a partnership," Simon later explained on *The X Factor Australia.* "It was only going to work if we listened to each other. It wasn't about me making them do things they were uncomfortable with. They listened to me and, more importantly, I listened to them."

For the next few days, they would be booked into a hotel in London because they had gigs and interviews lined up. It felt odd outside the cocoon of *The X Factor*, but they had the comfort of Simon there for them. He told them that if he wasn't there in person then they could phone him anytime they wanted.

One Direction soon came to relish the freedom of being away from the regimented routine and pressure of the show, and they became increasingly excited about what the future held for them. Their biggest fear earlier in the competition was that they'd just have to go back to where they came from. But now it was clear that wasn't going to happen. They had already built a huge fanbase and their support on Twitter remained solid, with people telling them they *must* stay together. They had everything to play for.

The winner of the very first *X Factor* had also aired his views on Twitter, and they were not so encouraging.

Steve Brookstein's career had flopped after his triumph six years earlier. Initially, all seemed well when, having secured a record contract with Cowell's Syco Music, his first single, a cover of Phil Collins' 'Against All Odds', went to number one in the UK charts and his debut album was also a chart topper. However, unhappy about recording covers, Steve fell out with Simon after arguing that he wanted to record his own songs. Nine months after winning *The X Factor*, he was dropped by the record company. Since then he has been performing in small venues around the country – his once promising career prospects now appearing rather bleak.

Several barbed comments and accusations passed between the two men over the following years. "It's amazing how many doors close when you part company with Cowell," Brookstein has said. "It's almost like leaving a mafia family. Simon Cowell has such an enormous ego. He believes that if he can't make you a star, then no one will." He also called Cowell a "leech" and "not a nice man".

Simon took the opportunity to really stick the boot in at a hospice fundraising event at London's Dorchester Hotel. In a Q&A with seriously ill children, he was asked to name the worst person he had dealt with on the show. He named Steve. "He was horrible, ungrateful and totally selfish," he replied. "He just wouldn't listen."

Now a frustrated Steve Brookstein turned towards Syco signing Louis Tomlinson, to let fly with some scathing comments. He tweeted Louis directly, saying: "You have a great opportunity. Take singing lessons and become a proper singer. Work on your breathing and support."

Later, he wrote on his own Twitter account: "After seeing Louis Tomlinson's audition I feel for all those young talented kids learning their craft. Seems you don't need talent any more."

Louis' mother, Jay, took to Twitter to defend her son, asking Brookstein why he was being "so cruel".

"Hi, I'm Louis' mum. My family have always liked you and bought your records. Why be so cruel? Why shame him in public?"

Whether or not Louis welcomed his mum's intervention is debatable, because she went on to embarrass him somewhat.

"He was sad about his audition. He was incredibly nervous. He is 18, Steve! I honestly thought you were a nice bloke. Sadly for us now what we were told about you seems accurate."

Far from contrite, Brookstein replied: 'If you are Louis' mum, get the poor lad some singing lessons for Christmas. A couple of dozen at least.'

The war of words continued in a clash on the Sheffield radio show *Juice FM*, where both had been invited to air their opinions. Brookstein apologised for giving an opinion which he knew Louis' mother might find "a little bit harsh".

But Jay felt he had been unnecessarily rude and critical of her son, and she was going to let him know it. "It wasn't just that – I actually liked you as a person," she said. "I bought your records, I watched you on *X Factor* when you won. I voted for you. So to be quite honest it was an utter shock, because I don't know why you personally picked one person out.

"You could have thought those thoughts to yourself, rather than actually invite a lot of people to start some kind of campaign against Louis. Let's face it, he will know that he's vocally the weakest in the group.

"Now, if you've ever felt like that about something you don't need somebody to point that out to you. But, as you've seen, you've had a thousand people tweeting back what a prat you are, so I'm sure you do feel a prick."

But neither was backing down. He replied, "Listen. You've got loads of these acts who are shown up and humiliated on *The X Factor*. They're terrible."

Referring to a female duo – Abby and Lisa, aka Ablisa – who had argued onstage before hitting each other, he continued, "You're a bit hypocritical to accept that it's OK for a TV show to humiliate young girls who punch each other on TV. You've got a guy dressed up as Michael Jackson who's not that good, but just because your son gets through – and he happens to be not as good… and he's worse than Wagner."

Jay replied: "Those people who went on – the punching girls – they were invited back on. They were given the choice: 'Do you want to earn a bit of money for a bit of a laugh?' And that's what they've done.

"They weren't humiliated as such. We've all watched them. I met both those girls backstage and they've been really nice girls. They knew that they made a mistake, and what they did is use it to their advantage."

★ ★ ★

The next few days after signing were a mass of various club gigs and management meetings. Everywhere they went, One Direction were amazed by the reception they received. Then it was time to go home for Christmas. They had all received £8,000 each on signing to Simon Cowell's Syco label, which was more money than they ever had in their lives.

Back home, Harry felt uncomfortable about a group of fans standing outside his family's house; as it was so cold outside, he went out to see them and say hello every now and then. School was now on hold for Niall, who was planning to move to London. One of the first things he did when he returned home was to tuck into a beef sandwich and fries at his local Supermac's – Ireland's largest fast food chain – and visit the Spar supermarket where he'd previously undertaken work experience.

Niall divided his time over the festive period between his father, Bobby's, home in Mullingar and mother, Maura's, in Longford. With a record deal under his belt and a management company to look after him, Liam felt financially secure enough to splash out on Christmas presents for his family. He bought four iPads, a laptop, a phone for his mum's birthday and some expensive bracelets. He also took his family out to dinner and bought a friend some trainers. Louis also enjoyed being able to splash the cash on his family for the first time.

The boys kept in touch over Christmas by text, with Harry and Louis speaking on the telephone a few times. Louis was delighted when Niall phoned him on Christmas Eve to wish him a happy birthday.

All of the boys had to come to terms with the fact that people would follow them around, ask for autographs and ask them questions when they were out in public – which made Christmas shopping a tricky, drawn-out affair.

Niall chilled out so much back home that he spent much of the time sleeping. Normally, he was the first in the family to get up on Christmas Day, but he was so exhausted that he didn't get out of bed until 11 a.m. He went to visit his mum for lunch and then came back home to his dad's, for a second dinner with all of the family. On New Year's Eve, he went out drinking with friends and inevitably found himself the centre of attention.

His childhood friend from Mullingar, Sean Cullen, with whom he has remained very close, noted, "He loves coming home." Niall's father, Bobby, concurred: "He can't wait to get back and see his family and friends. Despite his stardom, he hasn't changed. Niall hasn't lived at home since the day he left for that [*X Factor*] audition. And despite his international celebrity status, he still has his own bedroom, although it is at the bottom of the garden."

Zayn received an iPad for Christmas from his parents and, pleased to have some money to spend, treated his family in return. He bought his mother some jewellery and told his eldest sister, Doniya, that he would buy her the Ugg boots that she'd always wanted if she chose them herself. But he wasn't prepared for what happened when they went shopping together. One person recognised him and in the next moment a swarm of people thronged around him, wanting to say hello or to get his autograph.

Zayn had never been a big one for going out. He preferred spending time at home with his family or in his bedroom, playing computer games. But over the festive period he got a lot of invitations – including some from people that he didn't know that well. On New Year's Eve his friends persuaded him to go out with them, and he had such a wild night that he woke up on somebody's bathroom floor – at which point he got up and walked home.

But the New Year was to bring great sorrow into the Payne family, when Liam's sister Nicola's boyfriend died after a fight with a love rival. On New Year's Day, former soldier Craig Close was confronted by his best friend, Martin Gannon, an ex-boyfriend of Nicola's who had just discovered that Craig had slept with her. An argument broke out and Craig, 25, tragically died from a single punch to the head.

Craig and Martin, 24, had been next-door neighbours who had known each other since the age of five, and both were close to Liam's family. Both men had also accompanied Nicola to support Liam during his live *X Factor* performances in November and December. Martin Gannon was arrested, charged with manslaughter and subsequently given a prison sentence of two years and nine months.

★　★　★

Liam welcomed the opportunity to throw himself back into work later in January, when One Direction did a few gigs in Edinburgh, Leeds, Oxford and other cities. Then came the exciting news at a meeting with their management company that they would be going to Los Angeles in a few weeks to meet record producers and to start work on their debut album.

Arriving at LA Airport they were surprised to find a sizeable crowd had gathered to greet them, some holding a banner with 'One Direction' written on it. This was their first visit to the US as a group, but the power of the internet – including YouTube feeds of their *X Factor* performances – had prepared the way.

The boys stayed at the W hotel in LA, located between Rodeo Drive and the beaches of Santa Monica. Entering the foyer, they were impressed by the gold staircase, as was Harry by how polite and cheerful the hotel staff were compared with back home. This would also go for waiters and waitresses at the various restaurants they dined in.

Harry's own personal charm would not be enough when he approached a US TV reality star named Jillian Harris, 14 years his senior. She'd risen to fame after appearing on hit show *The Bachelor*, and was in LA to appear at a charity event and attend meetings about two possible new series. She was dining with a friend in the restaurant of the W Hotel, on a table next to One Direction.

Canadian-born Jillian didn't know who they were, but her friend did and pointed them out to her. When the pair of them got up to leave, Harry boldly walked over to her and said he would like to take her out for dinner.

Jillian thought him much too young for her and laughed, but Harry was not giving up. He told her he was playing a concert in Canada later in the year, and asked for her telephone number. She laughed and replied, "I am way too old for you." (Obviously she didn't know him!)

As Jillian later explained: "He looked cute and adorable but he was also very young looking. I could never date an 18-year-old. He didn't seem too put out. He was very sure of himself."

The boys made the most of the heated outdoor swimming pool at the hotel, and also took the opportunity to go shopping and stock up on some bargains. As they had all been given spending money, Harry had a spree in Abercrombie & Fitch; Louis teased him that he must have bought every T-shirt in the shop. Liam bought several pairs of trainers while Zayn focussed on the high-top models, because they were so much cheaper than in the UK. His favourite purchase was a pair of limited-edition, black Nike high-tops that cost $300. Back home his trainers remained in their boxes, to keep them in good shape; when he returned from LA, he kept his limited-edition high-tops in their box in his wardrobe – too scared to wear them! But it was Louis – who the others believe has a shopping addiction – who bought more than anyone else. Shirts, trousers, trainers – there was no stopping him.

In LA, One Direction recorded in the studio with producer-songwriter RedOne and his team, who has worked with the likes of Lady Gaga, Enrique Iglesias and Nicki Minaj. They also had dinner with writer-producer Max Martin, who has penned hits for Britney Spears, Pink, Katy Perry and Usher, amongst many others.

★   ★   ★

When One Direction had departed from the UK at Heathrow Airport's Terminal 3, they hadn't noticed all the fans mistakenly mustered at Terminal 5. But they were in for a shock when they returned, as they were mobbed by around 700 girls.

Unprepared, they ran into a car-parking booth where they hid. The police were called and attempted to hold back the excited crowd as the boys ran through. But Liam got hit in the face accidentally and some of the others had clothing ripped off. They were taken away in a police van, with flashing lights and a screaming siren.

Veteran boy-band member Ronan Keating, who sang with Boyzone, happened to be also arriving at Heathrow on the same flight as the boys. He later tweeted: "Just landed at Heathrow and when I walked out there were hundreds of screaming fans. Sadly not for me. Ha Ha. One Direction were on flight. X"

They may have only been together a few months, but such was the demand that they published their autobiography in February, entitled *One Direction: Forever Young.* Then it was back to *The X Factor.* Cleverly milking things for all their worth, Simon Cowell's annual live tour of the show's finalists was a big hit around the country. Matt Cardle might have won, but it was One Direction who attracted the most fans and the loudest screams where they appeared. There were girls with banners and T-shirts, declaring their love for the band, or for various members.

They played 51 dates around the UK's arenas and Matt Cardle was the final act, with five songs to sing. But there was little doubt that One Direction were the main event: they made the most dramatic entrance, rising from a hydraulically lifted stage in the centre of the arena, and they were the only other act who got to sing five songs. They chose 'Kids In America', 'Only Girl (In The World)', 'Chasing Cars' and 'Forever Young' – which they would have released as their winner's song, if they had been victorious in *The X Factor*. The finale had all the finalists singing 'Heroes', their chart-topping charity single.

During rehearsals for the tour, the boys were learning dance routines when they were embarrassed to be told by the choreographer to walk "a little sexily". Louis did a camp strut which had the others laughing.

They shared a dressing room with all the other male performers, but while most of them went to the bar after each show, Liam – who avoided alcohol because of his kidney deficiency – preferred to rest in his room. Louis, Harry and Zayn also sometimes skipped the bar and went to their rooms, but Niall could regularly be found there, chatting away to everyone.

"He was so lively and almost hyperactive," says a bar employee who has asked to remain anonymous. "He certainly enjoyed a drink and would have stayed up all night if his management hadn't eventually persuaded him to go to bed.

"He was quite loud but in a fun and cheerful way. Everyone liked him. He wasn't too big for his boots. Just like a normal young guy, really."

There had been intense pressure and a fair amount of competitive rivalry on *The X Factor*, but, now that it had ended, all the acts relaxed and enjoyed each other's company. Wagner proved particularly entertaining, with lots of amusing stories and jokes to tell.

In his hotel room, Liam always had a stage outfit laid out, ready to wear at a moment's notice. It was something he had been taught at home by his father, who made sure that he always had his clothes ready on the day before a performance. It was a professional approach to stop him worrying at the last minute.

While they were on *The X Factor*, One Direction provided a regular video diary on the show's website to keep their growing fanbase updated of what was going on in their lives, as well as an email Q&A session. Louis was always joking and playing the fool; when the boys were asked what they looked for in a girl, all gave serious answers apart from him, who replied, "I like a girl who eats carrots." It was just a silly throwaway line, but the comment was to haunt him for some time.

Fans started turning up at their gigs with carrot banners and real carrots to give to him. One night in Nottingham, he got into the spirit of things by wearing a carrot costume that a friend had given him for the finale of 'Heroes', while the others wore stuck-on beards and moustaches. They also got sent some mushrooms in a box with their faces painted on them. And Zayn was given a Borat-style mankini!

During the tour, Zayn began a romance with Rebecca Ferguson, who was six years older than him. He had been making overtures towards her while still in *The X Factor* competition, but she had resisted because she thought him too young. But Zayn persisted and, eventually, she fell completely in love with him. Rebecca, who had two children from a previous relationship, also introduced them to Zayn and they became mutually fond of each other.

For fun on tour, the boys occasionally dared each other to stick random words into the lyrics whilst singing on stage. Liam was challenged to say 'Rodney' and 'Del Boy' (characters from British TV comedy series *Only Fools & Horses*), while Niall had to insert 'combine harvester' and 'Ian Beale' (from British TV soap *EastEnders*) into several songs.

During the tour Liam had a problem with keeping his trousers intact. They kept ripping on stage; in Newcastle the tear was particularly large, stretching all the way from his crotch to mid-thigh, but he carried on singing and, at the end, gave an embarrassed smile!

At the end of the tour, Harry and his friend Johnny went on a skiing holiday to Courchevel, in France, with Louis and his pal Stan. Louis had never skied before but found it great fun. They got recognised quite a bit, but there was one embarrassing moment which they later saw the funny side of.

A male-female couple approached them and started gesturing towards them with their camera. Assuming they wanted to take a picture of them, Harry and Louis posed with their arms around each other but then the couple said, "No, we want you to take a photo of *us*."

Niall went to Spain with his dad, Bobby, and best friend, Sean. Zayn also went to Spain and Liam took his parents on holiday to Florida, where they visited Universal Studios. When they had been there on a previous holiday they didn't have a lot of money to spend, and so had to queue for a long time before going on any of the rides. But this time Liam was able to buy them all VIP passes, so they didn't have to wait any longer than five minutes.

Back in the UK, there was a series of signings around the country for their book, *Forever Young*, before heading for Sweden to work on their album in Stockholm. To their surprise, they found that their fame had spread to here too and a crowd of girls congregated outside their hotel, calling in English, "I love you!" and following them around.

During a book signing in Stockholm, one girl fan kept fainting every time she approached their desk. Security staff kept taking her outside for fresh air, but every time she approached them she fainted again – it happened four times!

★   ★   ★

In June 2011, Louis split with his girlfriend of 18 months, Hannah Walker. Shortly after, he paid a visit home to Doncaster and had a night out with old pal Stan. On the way home, they got chatting about the party island of Ibiza. Stan said he would really like to go and, on a whim, the pair of them decided to fly there for the weekend.

They flew out on a Friday evening and partied until the early hours of the following day, which they then spent relaxing – and recovering – before flying home.

Later that summer, One Direction crossed the Atlantic once more, heading for LA for three weeks for some more recording of the album and also to film the video for their debut single, which had been announced as 'What Makes You Beautiful'.

During the filming of the video, Louis was stopped by an LA cop for erratic driving. He thought the policeman had gestured to him to overtake and was indicating that he would follow behind, but he'd misinterpreted the signs. The cop was gesturing at him to pull over and, when Louis overtook him instead, wasn't best pleased!

Louis tried to calm him down and make light of it by saying, "Don't worry, mate. I'm not trying to race you." But the cop was stern and, with one hand on his gun, replied, "I will shut you down."

During a break, the boys took some girl fans to the amusement park on the pier in Santa Monica and rode on the spinning teacups. But this new, ever-moving lifestyle was taking its toll on their love lives as girlfriends were left behind. The next to split up were Zayn and Rebecca Ferguson in July.

"One day I just woke up and thought: 'This isn't working for me,'" Rebecca told *The Sun*. "I picked up the phone and called him and ended it. I said I didn't want the relationship any more. It was sad, but I wasn't feeling it."

Back in the UK Harry and Louis – whose close friendship earned them the joint name of 'Larry Stylinson' amongst fans – moved into an apartment together in London. They laughed at their so-called 'bromance' at first, but then began to tire of people talking about it so much that Louis tweeted it was "bullshit".

Louis' mum, Jay, and Harry's mum, Anne – who had also become friends – visited the house one weekend, along with Robin, and were shocked to find that the only thing they had to eat in the house was breakfast cereal.

★ ★ ★

'What Makes You Beautiful' was released on September 11, 2011 in the shops, but was available to download online the day before. To promote it, the boys went on a tour of HMV shops in the UK, signing copies of the CD. They travelled around in style by helicopter, and huge crowds turned out wherever they went.

Jay, who had bought the record as soon as it was in the shops, first heard that it had reached download number one in the UK charts when she was driving with her daughters in her car and heard the news on the radio. "We were all just screaming!" she told the *South Yorkshire Times*. "I tried to phone Louis but couldn't get hold of him until 7.10 p.m. When his sisters got on the school bus everyone cheered!"

Louis' younger twin sisters, Charlotte and Félicité, were big fans of One Direction and loved Louis being part of the group. They had their posters on the bedroom wall – but pride of place beside their beds was one of Harry and one of Simon!

Harry's penchant for older women shone through once more when the band was interviewed by attractive Emma Willis on British TV music show *The Hot Desk*. He was staring at her and looked besotted as the 35-year-old presenter – married to Matt Willis, former member of British band Busted, and seven months pregnant with their second child – looked a little flustered.

At one stage, when she asked them about who was the naughtiest in the group, she turned to Harry and said, "I imagine *you* do quite naughty things." He smiled and replied, "You have no idea."

In similar style, Harry seemed transfixed by broadcaster Lucy Horobin, when they headed to Manchester for a radio interview on Key 103. When she played 'What Makes You Beautiful', Harry stared at her like a wide-eyed puppy, holding his hand over his heart, miming along to the song and, as she turned away giggling, mouthing, "I love you."

At 32, she was nearly twice 17-year-old Harry's age, and seemed amused but flattered by his unexpected attention. After the show was over, the pair kept in touch via flirtatious text messages. A month later, when One Direction returned to her show and gave a live performance, the pair flirted shamelessly on air.

She introduced them by saying, "I'm joined by five very handsome boys and I've got you all to myself tonight."

"You look lovely today," flattered Harry, and a giggling Lucy replied, "Thanks Harry, so do you."

When the boys later joked that they were all moving in together, she asked who would be in charge of housework. Harry replied, "You can cook for us." When Lucy agreed, Harry remarked, "What a woman."

Niall was just days away from his 18th birthday, so Lucy presented him with a birthday cake, party poppers and musical horns, later mischievously telling Harry to "put your horn away". A former employee of the radio station recalls, "They had obviously been looking forward to seeing each other again. Both were being very flirtatious and some of their comments made the others in the band look a bit uncomfortable.

"Harry was completely enraptured by her and she was encouraging him with her comments. They were acting like lovesick teenagers which, in Harry's case, might have been true, but Lucy was not really being very professional."

Soon afterwards, they spent a night together at a hotel in Manchester. As Lucy had married Oliver Pope the previous summer, when her affair with Harry eventually came out it caused a scandal.

Liam's girlfriend, Danielle Peazer, on the other hand, was pleased to come out of the shadows when she accompanied him and his pals on a night out in London, where they celebrated Niall's birthday. They were joined by Aston and Marvin from JLS, who came second in *The X Factor* in 2008 and had since forged a successful career, as well as Marvin's pop-star girlfriend, Rochelle Wiseman, and her fellow girl-band singer in the Saturdays, Vanessa White. Actor James Corden was also there.

Initially, Liam had wanted to keep Danielle out of the public glare to protect her from the hassle and jealous comments, but she hadn't really understood his reasoning and resented it a little. However, when she did later experience some nasty comments from some girls on Twitter, she realised what he'd been doing

Harry was to play matchmaker for Louis that summer. He had met up for a drink with a friend of his from W. Mandeville Bakery, who brought along another friend, pretty student and part-time clothes model Eleanor Calder. Harry set her up on a date with Louis and they enjoyed a visit to the cinema to watch *The Inbetweeners Movie* together. Eleanor is a couple of years older than Louis and was about to start her second year at Manchester University, studying politics and sociology.

When they performed at London's G-A-Y club, Niall was again presented with a birthday cake but it resulted in a cake fight. The boys decided to share it with the audience by throwing chunks of it into the crowd. It all got a bit messy onstage and Harry slipped over mid-performance.

★   ★   ★

With what 'What Makes You Beautiful' at number one in the UK charts and the internet spreading their fame ever wider, they went to visit their fans abroad on the Bring 1D To Me Tour. It was a hectic five-day visit to Stockholm, Milan, Munich and Amsterdam, meeting fans and answering their questions.

Their first stop was the beautiful Café Opera in Stockholm, located in the Opera House, where, in a taste of what was to come, they arrived to find fans queuing around the block.

In Milan, hundreds of fans started singing 'What Makes You Beautiful' when the boys arrived. At one stage, Italian riot police were called in to protect them from the crowd. But Harry did take the opportunity to swap phone numbers with one girl. As Louis was later to remark: "Everyone said about Swedish women being hot and I have to agree, but we'd been in Italy for about 20 minutes and every woman we saw was phenomenal."

Back in Britain, Zayn revealed he had a crush on the new *X Factor* judge, N-Dubz singer Tulisa. At a launch for a new mobile phone he told reporters, "She just looks so hot. Someone needs to give her my number, tell her to call me."

For Niall's birthday, however, the rest of the boys bought him a life-sized waxwork of US President Barack Obama – a politician he particularly admired. Niall had explained to them that he'd "fallen in love" with him after he visited Ireland and gave a speech, so they'd arranged for the model to be specially made and delivered to him.

Niall was delighted and joked that maybe next year, he could get the President's wife, Michelle, too. Niall kept the model on a bench at his apartment in north London, later moving it to the balcony where it got some odd looks from passers-by down below.

At the after-show party for the conclusion of that year's *X Factor*, Harry snogged *Xtra Factor* host Caroline Flack, 31, at the W Hotel in London. Afterwards, they left in a cab together. Harry had been open about the fact that he fancied her. In August he'd told the official *X Factor* website: "If Caroline Flack is reading this, say 'Hi' from me. She is gorgeous!"

He even got Tim Dean, producer of *Xtra Factor*, to send tweets to Caroline the following month to persuade her to date him. One read: "I think you should consider dating @HarryStyles he's oh so handsome + charismatic and defo not sat next to me now!"

Harry, who is 15 years her junior, posted a picture on Twitter of himself holding a message that read: "To Flackster! Never too old… Let's make it happen!! Lots of Love Harry S."

Harry would later be a frequent overnight visitor to her home in north London and they regularly dined out at restaurants together. After much media speculation about whether or not they were dating – or just friends – Caroline broke her silence in an interview with *Now* magazine.

She revealed that she had received death threats on Twitter from diehard One Direction fans, warning her to steer clear of their idol. She put it down to people not accepting the age gap between them.

"I feel like I shouldn't have to worry about what I do," she said. "But it's a social thing that people aren't accepting of big age gaps. I keep thinking, 'What have I done wrong?' But I haven't done anything wrong. What's hard for me to get my head around is people saying it's disgusting. I don't think it is. If two people like each other and get on, why does anyone else find a negative in it?"

Caroline went on to say how Harry had become the mature one in their relationship, on account of being so supportive and telling her not to take any notice of the remarks on Twitter. "It's a form of bullying from people who are hiding behind a computer," she added. "I knew they were just a minority of One Direction fans and all very young – it's a kind of fanatical obsession."

Meanwhile, when Harry was interviewed on US website *Showbiz 411*, he was asked what his age limit was when he came to dating women. Harry didn't look like he wanted to answer but, egged on by the others, he replied, "I wouldn't go any older than my mum. She's 44."

While Harry was increasingly gaining a reputation as a Lothario, his flatmate Louis was amused by all the comings and goings at their home. "The worst thing about living with Harry is the constant stream of women he is getting through our door. It's relentless," he joked to *The Sun*. "I am a one-woman man with Eleanor. It's still not quite official. We haven't put a name on it but I really like her, she's cool. The good thing is everyone has been so nice about it. If the fans see her they ask her for a photo and she gets shy."

The good side, he said, was that Harry was a decent cook and would make them Mexican dishes like fajitas and tacos. Louis was a complete novice at cooking but did try his hand at creating a romantic meal for Eleanor. It was the first meal he had ever cooked for anyone: chicken breast wrapped in ham, with homemade mashed potatoes and gravy.

The other boys – Niall, Zayn and Liam – all had separate apartments in the same north London block of flats, giving them plenty of opportunity to play pranks on each other. On one occasion, Niall and Louis locked Harry in a wardrobe and walked off. While he was in there Harry, typically, took all his clothes off and when they returned to let him out, they were greeting with a naked Styles announcing, "Ta-dah!"

Another time, while staying at a hotel, Harry and Louis went swimming in their underwear in the morning and woke Niall up by flinging their dripping wet undies onto his face! As Harry observed: "We are not polished and well behaved. We're just like the cheeky guys you know at school – nothing's really changed!"

One night at a hotel, Louis started sleepwalking and got into Niall's bed. A started Niall pushed him onto the floor and he sat up, put his arms out and started humming 'The Bare Necessities' from Disney's *The Jungle Book*!

Liam jumped at the chance to dress as his favourite superhero character, Batman, at a fancy dress party to celebrate his sister Nicola's 21st birthday. But despite his fame and wealth, he still took heed of his mum, Karen, who balked at how much he was prepared to spend on the outfit; he'd found one online for £500 but Karen said he was "mad", so instead he bought one for £50.

One Direction returned to *The X Factor* to perform alongside pop queen Lady Gaga in November, and met up with girl-band contestants Little Mix. One in particular caught Zayn's eye: Perrie Edwards. He told the other lads that he thought she was "very cute."

Later, on *The Xtra Factor* there were several awkward moments when the boys went on to talk to co-presenters Olly Murs and Caroline Flack. Harry strolled on with a large bouquet of flowers as the hosts stood to greet the band – and promptly presented them to Olly, along with a kiss.

"Harry, thank you so much for the flowers," a mischievous Olly replied. Then, turning towards Caroline, Olly added, "And I got a kiss. Snap!" He then gave her a high-five.

It was Harry's way of trying to make a joke of all the gossip surrounding him and Caroline, but it was clear that the pair of them felt uncomfortable together in the limelight. Trying to be professional, Caroline asked each one of the boys in turn whether they thought that contestant Kitty Brucknell – who was in the over-25s category – had been the right person to be eliminated that evening. Harry, sitting closest to her, was the last to speak, looking down at the floor as Caroline prompted him: "Harry, you are a Kitty fan, aren't you?"

He looked at her with a sheepish grin but, before he could say anything, Olly interjected, "You like the older category, don't you?" As the others – particularly Niall – fell about laughing, Harry joined in with the fun. "Yeah, I like the 'overs'."

Caroline chuckled and then said, "Next!"

But there was more teasing to come. Referring to the remaining *X Factor* contestants, Olly asked, "Harry, which girl do you fancy the most?" Quick as a flash, Louis said, "Caroline!"

Again there were laughs all round, and more to come when a smirking Harry said, "They are all a bit young for me."

Olly asked them who was the nicest of the acts they had met, and Zayn replied, "Little Mix." Knowing that Zayn fancied Perrie, Harry leaned forward, happy to be teasing for a change: "What do you think of Little Mix, Zayn?" he asked.

When Caroline said, "You are a fan of Little Mix, aren't you Zayn?" Harry looked at her and asked, "How do you know?"

As Louis chuckled, Zayn tried to be serious and impartial. "It's the way they have progressed since they were put together as a group, in terms of their vocal ability and how they have gelled. They seem really good friends. That's hard to do on a show like this. They've done really well and I think we're behind them."

Niall added, "They remind me of us, when we were on the show."

Caroline, who must either have heard or noticed the frisson between Zayn and Perrie, then mischievously asked, "Do you have a favourite member of Little Mix… Zayn?"

He shuffled in his seat and replied, "No, no. I like them all equal."

But Harry, presumably happy to no longer be the focus of the interview, bluntly asserted, "Zayn likes Perrie."

★   ★   ★

A few weeks later, Harry was surprised to get a text from his mother saying, "I didn't know you were moving." When he asked what she was talking about, she told him she'd read in a newspaper that he was moving in with Caroline Flack. Harry assured her that he wasn't, and when Louis found out he jokingly pretended to cry: "But you're living with me!"

One Direction's second single, 'Gotta Be You', reached number three in the UK charts when hit machine Rihanna was at the top with 'We Found Love'. Their debut album, *Up All Night*, reached number two. One of the songs on the album, 'Moments', was written by A Team singer Ed Sheeran, who would become a friend of the boys.

In late 2011, One Direction signed a big money deal with the giant Columbia Records to launch a US promotional tour the following year. "America is a massive place and it's going to be hard," Harry told newspaper reporters in the UK. "A lot of people have tried and failed but we want to break the mould and see what we can do. We'll definitely give it a go."

Later in November they scooped three awards at the 4Music Video Honours, organised by Channel 4 Television: Best Group, Best Breakthrough and Best Video.

Always keen to get back to Ireland, Niall welcomed the chance the fly to Dublin with his colleagues to appear on popular chat series *The Late Late Show*. Genial host Ryan Tubridy showed them the dolls modelled on One Direction, which caused much amusement. Harry remarked, "Mine looks like Susan Boyle." (The middle-aged spinster had been a sensation on *Britain's Got Talent* in 2009, when she sang 'I Dreamed A Dream' from *Les Misérables*.)

Niall was in particularly good form, pleased to be back on home ground. His mother and grandmother had come along to watch the show. But it wasn't just them who were proud of him. It seemed that much of Ireland had taken him to its heart. Ryan mentioned that there were three or four hundred fans behind the barriers when they arrived, and asked how they were dealing with this "new life".

"It's insane," Harry replied. "We are learning to cope with it but we're just normal guys and it's such a strange thing to have happened to us." But he was squirming in his seat when Ryan asked him about the "slightly older lady – Caroline Flack" that he had been linked with.

"We're just really good friends," came his response. "We get on well. She's a really nice person."

As the others glanced at him with some amusement, Ryan teased, "So, you're just good friends?"

"Who knows? We'll see what happens," said Harry.

But Ryan wasn't giving up and kept asking if he fancied her.

Harry admitted, "I think she's very hot. She's an attractive lady."

Later they performed 'What Makes You Beautiful', which received a rousing reception.

Towards the end of the month, One Direction began filming the video for their third single, 'One Thing', in central London. Many fans turned out to watch as they hit the landmarks, including Trafalgar Square and Covent Garden, and messed around on the top of a red double-decker bus.

At that year's Capital Radio Jingle Bell Ball, on December 4, they joined a line-up that included JLS, Emeli Sandé, Ed Sheeran and the Saturdays to perform three songs before a huge crowd at London's O₂ Arena: 'Gotta Be You', 'One Thing' and 'What Makes You Beautiful'.

In an interview on Capital FM in advance of the show, the boys were asked about their favourite sandwich, and gave some interesting answers. Harry's was pretty standard fare: ham with Branston pickle. But Louis wasn't interested in any contrast of flavours in the filling, excitedly replying, "prawn, with prawn mayo and prawn crisps", which he insisted was "wicked". Zayn, who had been shaking his head throughout, thought a "12-inch chicken sensation" could not be beaten.

And when it came to the notion of inventing a new flavoured ice cream, Louis had them all screwing up their faces in disgust when he suggested "Yorkshire Tea ice cream."

Liam looked at him and commented, "You're weird."

Just before Christmas, One Direction kicked off their eagerly awaited first UK tour in Liam's home town of Wolverhampton, where they were watched by 2,500 fans. The boys were amazed to find a hot tub and a sauna in their dressing room, clambering into the tub before going onstage.

The show was split into three seasonally themed sections. On a screen behind them, summer was represented by the band surfing and fooling about on a beach; autumn showed them returning to school, and in the winter they were holed up in a log cabin eating lumpy porridge in thick-knit novelty jumpers.

They opened the show with the uptempo 'Na Na Na', which got the audience even more excited than they already were. Other numbers included 'Stand Up', 'Gotta Be You' and covers including 'I Gotta Feeling', 'Stereo Hearts' and 'Valerie'. They ended with the crowd-pleasing 'What Makes You Beautiful' and 'I Want'.

But they were to be a smash hit of a different sort when they moved on to Birmingham in the New Year. A car rammed the back of their tour bus after the show, leaving them all shaken. Police and ambulance crews were called to the scene and, despite three of them complaining of back pains and headaches, they were fit enough to continue the tour at their next destination, Plymouth.

One fan in Nottingham had an unusual way of showing her appreciation, after the band finished singing 'What Makes You Beautiful'. She hurled several tampons at Harry – one of which hit him in the face!

When they played London's Hammersmith Apollo, Caroline Flack came to watch them. By then, however, her romance with Harry was coming to an end.

Meanwhile, the boys were delighted to be nominated for a prize at the forthcoming Brit Awards – the country's more prestigious music honours. They were up for Best Single for 'What Makes You Beautiful', and over 14,000 fans greeted them at Dublin's O$_2$ Arena, where tickets had sold out within minutes of being on sale.

Niall was determined to introduce the others to some fine Irish food while they were there, and so he got his mother, Maura, to bring along some Clonakilty sausages, telling them that they would never have tasted sausages that good before.

The boys agreed that their Irish fans were amongst the craziest – screaming for them as soon as they touched down at the airport and barely stopping until they had left the country! As Niall explained, "The fans here like the fact that there's an Irish person in a British based band, which is good. And I'm as common as muck, so I suppose they can relate to me."

Around 30 family and friends from Mullingar came to watch Niall perform. As fans milled outside their hotel, most of the boys stayed in for a rest – apart from Niall, who went shopping. Harry joked, "He is a diva now because he's back at home but we will keep him under control."

Backstage, Niall got chatting to attractive Irish TV presenter Glenda Gilson, and was surprised at how tall she was. But that didn't stop him cheekily asking the 31-year-old presenter for a date on Twitter the following day. The pair became good friends and would meet up occasionally in the future, whenever they could – but that was apparently all it was, not a romance.

Afterwards, the boys boarded a bus to Belfast for their final tour dates. But there would be little time for a rest before they flew out to LA on a promotional tour to pave the way for a series of US gigs at the end of February, when they would be supporting a boy band put together by US TV channel Nickelodeon.

One Direction flew out from Belfast to Heathrow on January 27, 2012, and then onto LA. Hundreds of fans were waiting for them at LAX airport, but the security staff told them that it wasn't safe for them to greet their fans and so they were rushed through. Harry and Niall subsequently took to Twitter to apologise directly for not saying hello.

Hundreds more fans were camped outside their hotel and the boys were forced to use the hotel's service elevator, because a string of girls were going up and down in the main elevator throughout their stay, hoping to bump into them. When they emerged from the hotel, a huge crowd of girls screamed for them. Harry and Louis took a tannoy from one of the security staff to try to talk to them, but were unable to be heard above the screams.

Remarkably, they had yet to release any records in the US. But presales of their album were huge.

They headed to the Nickelodeon studios, where they were to film an episode of teen sitcom *iCarly*. The daughter of former bodybuilder turned action movie star (turned governor of California) Arnold Schwarzenegger had set her sights on Harry, requesting tickets to watch the recording of the show. Afterwards, Katherine Schwarzenegger introduced herself. Harry wasn't interested romantically, but joked to the others later that he was wary of hard man Arnie.

"Imagine having Arnie as your dad-in-law," he said. Doing a passable impression of the Austrian-born *Terminator* star, he mimicked, "Leave my house if you want to live."

The previous day, Katherine had tweeted: "Just watched my first One Direction video with my cousin and @Harry Styles is a cutie indeed!"

The premise of the TV series is that teenager Carly Shay, played by Miranda Cosgrove, creates her own web show, called *iCarly*, with best friends Sam Puckett and Freddie Benson. One Direction were to play themselves in guest roles in a story which sees Carly getting sick with 'jungle worms' after a holiday. When One Direction agree to appear on her show, Harry also gets the sickness after drinking from her water bottle. When he isn't better after a week, the others suspect that he is just faking his illness, enjoying lying in bed and having Carly take care of him. In order to get him to confess, they pretend that they want to accept Gibby, a huge One Direction fan, into the band in his absence. Harry is so shocked by the idea that he stops pretending to be sick and One Direction perform 'What Makes You Beautiful'.

It was a brief visit to the US, but it had heightened their profile for the return in a few weeks' time.

Back in London for a rest, Harry enjoyed socialising in London's West End with celebrity pals including James Corden and Radio 1 DJ Nick Grimshaw. He also got friendly with 28-year-old TV presenter Alexa Chung. But when newspapers speculated about their relationship, she tweeted, "Sorry to all the 1D fans who followed me for Harry updates. WE ARE NOT DATING. He did make me cheese on toast though, which was pretty sexy."

In an interview with the website *Sugarscape*, Liam likened being in the band to being at school: "When we have stopped working it's like break time at school. You just get to hang around with your mates."

A brief visit to Paris via Eurostar got quite scary for One Direction, as they were mobbed at Gare Du Nord train station. It took a joint effort by police and army to manage to hold the crowd back enough so that the boys could squeeze their way through. But such was the clamour that Liam lost a shoe – much to Harry's amusement!

At the Brits, held at London's O$_2$ Arena, they won Best British Single for 'What Makes You Beautiful' in a public vote, ahead of such other hits as Adele's 'Someone Like You', Ed Sheeran's 'The A Team' and Jessie J featuring B.O.B with 'Price Tag'.

The group dedicated the award to their fans, with Harry adding, "Everything we do is for you, and this is yours." They celebrated their success in a very un-star like manner by scoffing burgers in the nearest McDonald's, while record label bosses waited for them at the after party. As Niall later explained, "The Brits food was amazing but the portions were so small."

Their success left them in great spirits as they travelled to Heathrow Airport three days later, on their quest to crack America.

# 10

# American Beauties

Riding high on the back of One Direction's success at the Brit Awards, the single 'What Makes You Beautiful' made the highest debut for a UK act in the US singles chart for 14 years. Over 100,000 copies were downloaded before it was even played on the radio in America.

At this time, the boys were supporting American boy band Big Time Rush for some of their gigs across North America. One Direction's management continued to show just how adept they were at promotion, via the internet: when tickets went on sale, they asked American fans to vote for which city they would like One Direction to visit in a meet-and-greet marketing campaign entitled Bring 1D To US. Their album would also be released in the United States mid-March, days after their tour ended.

Thousands of screaming fans descended on Chicago as One Direction landed at O'Hare International airport for their first US gig, which took place at the Rosemont Theatre. Several newspapers and news channels were later to compare it to the arrival of four other cheeky, fresh-faced Brits nearly 50 years earlier, when the Beatles first landed at Kennedy Airport in 1964 and 3,000 screaming fans were waiting for them.

One Direction might have been the support act, but it soon became clear that most of the fans in the audience were there for them. In fact, around 200 people left before the main act and this trend continued throughout the tour, which saw them play in Chicago, Detroit, Toronto, Albany, Connecticut, Virginia, Boston, Durham, Nashville and finally New York City, at the famous Radio City Music Hall.

"We didn't expect anyone to really know who we were when we came out here but the support has been amazing," Zayn later told *The David Letterman Show*.

They kicked off their set with 'I Want', followed by 'Moments', a cover of Kings Of Leon's 'Use Somebody', 'More Than This', 'One Thing', 'Up All Night' and, finally, 'What Makes You Beautiful'. The crowd sang along word-perfect to every song, despite the fact the band's album was yet to be released in the US.

The stage design was workmanlike at best, and it looked like every expense had been spared. A rather sorry-looking black curtain with the group's name emblazoned in white letters served as the backdrop, and that was pretty much it. Not that their fans minded. They were in such a state of exhilaration that when a stage hand walked on to place some bottles of water on the floor, he was greeted with screams of excitement! In an echo of the Beatles' early US performances, the deafening crescendo of screams all but drowned out their vocals from near-hysterical fans.

When they moved on to Toronto, thousands lined the streets and city officials had to close roads as One Direction made their first ever appearance on Canadian TV. Outside the studio, a large crowd had to be kept back by police barriers. As the boys made their way inside, a pink bra was thrown at them! The chaos was only marginally less inside; as they struggled to be heard in an interview on the *Much Music* show, the screaming (mostly female) audience drowned out their replies. Incredibly, their fans outnumbered Justin Bieber's when he last appeared on the show: there were 17,000 requests for tickets from One Direction fans, compared with 4,000 for Canadian-born Bieber. Their appearance on US national radio station Z100 also attracted 15,000 questions on Twitter, three and a half times the amount Bieber had on the show.

It was on Toronto TV channel YTV that they revealed what they got up to in the dressing room, just prior to performing on stage. "We just mess about," said Zayn. "We have this game called Real Fruit Ninja and basically you throw a piece of fruit in the air and you cut it in half with a knife." Then, realising this was a potentially very dangerous activity and not wanting their many young fans to try it, he was prompted by the others to add, "But don't try this at home." Liam explained that the game developed because of the similarity of dressing rooms the whole world over: "Every dressing room we go in just seems to have a chopping board, a knife and a bowl of fruit. And that's it."

Another game they played while touring was far more mundane. They had all played Monopoly in their childhood but had rediscovered the attraction on the road. They were all agreed that Liam was the most competitive one in the band when it came to any kind of game. Even Liam said he had always been competitive – right back to his schooldays and any sporting activity.

When asked about the best piece of advice they had been given, they were again agreed. "'Uncle' Simon Cowell told us to go out there and just be the band that we want to be and that's what we do every day," said Liam.

When they performed at Toronto's Air Canada Centre, by far the greater number of fans in the 6,000-strong crowd was wearing One Direction T-shirts rather than Big Time Rush (and once more, a sizeable portion left after One Direction finished their set). Back in the US, fans in Dallas were overjoyed when their city won the Bring 1D To US competition. The band would be visiting on March 24, 2012.

Meanwhile, on the other side of the Atlantic, tickets for their 2013 UK arena tour sold out in minutes and extra dates were quickly added.

★   ★   ★

Midway through the North American tour, Zayn – who had already lost his grandfather during *The X Factor* – received yet more sad news from back home. His aunt had died, and so he flew home for her funeral.

Harry tweeted to fans: "Our thoughts are with him and his family at this sad time." He missed three gigs, in Connecticut, Virginia and Boston.

The rest of them had to sing Zayn's lines onstage. Because they were unused to doing it, it did cause some confusion, with both Liam and Harry singing his line together at one point.

There was a lot of travelling involved on the tour, but the boys loved the plush tour bus. They were all football fans, so much time on the road was spent playing the FIFA football game on Playstation, and Louis had a generous supply of his beloved Yorkshire tea with him to keep him happy.

Harry had a sore throat during the tour and all the boys were feeling run-down, so they all had regular vitamin jabs. Added to which, Harry was also feeling quite homesick.

But they enjoyed the large portions of food they got in restaurants and fast-food outlets in the States, compared to the more modest sizes back home. Even Niall, who had the biggest appetite, was satisfied. But Harry had developed a reputation as a 'food scrounger'. He would always be pinching chips or burgers, or pretty much anything else, from the others' plates after he had finished his own, which was a little irritating for them.

The weather occasionally reminded them of home though. In Boston, one 16-year-old girl fan was disappointed it was raining, explaining to a newspaper reporter: "It might mean that One Direction won't like the city and they'll never, ever come back again." Another fan remarked: "I love their hair. They have voices like angels, even though they are just ordinary boys." When they did a brief meet-and-greet with fans in Boston, five girls came dressed as each member of the band, which the boys found hilarious.

After their final gig at New York's famous Radio City Hall, they were stuck in their tour bus for half an hour after it stopped at traffic lights. Over 100 fans swarmed around the vehicle, banging the sides and climbing onto the roof. Niall joked that one girl was "like an Olympic sprinter" because she kept up with them for about five blocks all the way to their hotel. Talking about the gig, Harry said: "It was definitely the loudest place we've ever played. The noise levels were incredible."

116

Niall has fun on El Hormiguero TV show at Vertice Studio, Madrid, October 31, 2012. JUAN NAHARRO GIMENEZ/GETTY IMAGES

Liam shows off his tattoos during Z100's *Jingle Ball* 2012, at Madison Square Garden, New York, December 7, 2012.

Harry works the crowd into a frenzy at the *Radio One Teen Awards* at Wembley Arena, London, October 7, 2012.
MIKE MARSLAND/WIREIMAGE

Niall onstage during Z100's *Jingle Ball* 2012, presented by Aeropostale, at Madison Square Garden, New York, December 7, 2012. KEVIN MAZUR/GETTY IMAGES FOR JINGLE BALL 2012

Singing in front of traditional red British telephone boxes to near hysterical fans on NBC's *Today* at Rockefeller Plaza, New York, November 13, 2012. KEVIN MAZUR/WIREIMAGE

A 'suitable' occasion at *The Brit Awards* 2012 at The O2 Arena, London, February 21, 2012. DAVE HOGAN/GETTY IMAGES

The boys accept the Best Pop Video award onstage during the 2012 *MTV Video Music Awards* at Staples Center, Los Angeles, September 6, 2012. KEVIN WINTER/GETTY IMAGES

The jubilant boys accept their Global Success Award at *The Brit Awards* 2013 at The O2 Arena in London, February 20, 20
DAVE J HOGAN/GETTY IMAGES

Louis is dressed to impress at the *BRIT Awards* 2013 at the O2 Arena in London, February 20, 2013.
DAVE M. BENETT/GETTY IMAGES

It all kicks off at *The Brit Awards* 2013 at 02 Arena, London, February 20, 2013.
DAVE J HOGAN/GETTY IMAGES

Simon Cowell had spoken to the boys on the phone from Britain, telling them he was so excited by the reaction they were getting in the US that he couldn't sleep. Harry told the *Daily Mirror:* "For us to even be here and have this kind of reaction is just incredible. People are being so, so nice and welcomed us so much, and for them to have taken the interest that they have in us feels pretty special."

Such was the hysteria – no British band had found America so easy to conquer since the Beatles – that even the upmarket broadsheet newspapers back in the UK had to take notice. *The Guardian* sent an interviewer out to their final gig at Radio City, who was taken aback to see Harry bending over with his trousers and Calvin Kleins down, saying, "My bum's ready" – it was for the doctor to administer a vitamin shot.

Later that evening, they celebrated their remarkable invasion of North America rather too forcefully at a bowling alley. Still high on adrenalin from the gig hours earlier, they started bowling two and three balls at a time down a lane – and ended up smashing the machinery.

On radio station Z100, they gave an update on their current celebrity crushes. Liam still fancied Leona Lewis and Niall chose Demi Lovato, while Harry went for Kate Beckinsale, Louis for Natalie Portman and Zayn for model-turned-actress Rosie Huntington-Whiteley. When asked who their biggest musical influence was, three of them – Zayn, Louis and Niall – named Bruno Mars, Liam plumped for Justin Timberlake and Harry said Coldplay frontman Chris Martin.

Harry also had a thing for reality TV star Kim Kardashian. While being filmed at Q102 radio station in Pennsylvania, he picked up a large poster of Kardashian in a bikini and stuck a Post-it note to it that said, "Call me, maybe."

Niall's mum, Maura, had come out to see him in New York and stayed for a couple of weeks. She was startled when she walked through Radio City after the gig, being surrounded by fans eager to have their photograph taken with her.

"It makes me very emotional seeing what he's doing, it really is changing his life – it's so huge," she said. "What else could a mother ask for her child? I always warn him to be nice to the girls and always chat to them and pose for pictures."

Niall proved particularly popular in New York, which was put down to the sizeable number of New Yorkers who come from an Irish background. He was presented with many Irish flags, hats and leprechaun dolls.

Louis was over the moon when girlfriend Eleanor flew out to join him in New York after five days. She joined him, his stepsisters Lottie and Félicité and his grandparents for a meal at the Trattoria Trecolori Italian restaurant in Times Square.

Before flying home, they performed live on *The Today Show* at New York's Rockefeller Plaza. They arrived on an open-topped, red London double-decker bus, waving from the top to 10,000 screaming fans. Amongst the home-made banners in the crowd, some read, "Niall will you go to prom with me?" or "Zayn + Michelle = prom". They sang three tracks: 'What Makes You Beautiful', 'One Thing' and 'More Than This'.

*Up All Night* was released in the US the following day – with perfect timing. It charted at number 28 and then went to number one a few days later. They were the first British pop band to have a number one in the US with a debut album, beating the Spice Girls' achievement when their debut, *Spice*, went in at number six in 1997.

News that it had reached number one came when the boys had a few days off. Niall was in the back of a cab, en route to buying some tickets for himself and Liam to watch a New York Knicks basketball game when someone from the band's management company rang to inform him. The news was delivered in the best tradition of Simon Cowell on *The X Factor*: "It's close," he said. "We've got the numbers... [dramatic pause] ... but you've got number one." Niall was so excited that he screamed with delight, startling the cab driver.

When Zayn phoned home to tell his mum about the album going to number one, Tricia started crying with happiness.

Back in Britain, Simon Cowell commented, "It is an incredible achievement. They deserve it. They have the best fans in the world."

The album also topped the charts in Italy, Sweden, Singapore, Hong Kong, Thailand and the Philippines. It was number two in New Zealand

and Ireland, number three in the UAE and Portugal, Top 5 in Spain, Finland and Australia and Top 10 in five other countries.

Back home in Ireland, Niall's dad, Bobby, told the *Irish Sun* he was in shock at the level of his son's success. "It is absolutely fantastic, I can't believe it," he said. "It's big news with the boys every week. We never thought he would be this successful. We thought he'd be back here after a couple of months with his tail between his legs, but we are so proud."

Referring to them shooting to the top of the US charts, he added, "None of the major acts have done this, not the Beatles, not Coldplay. I wouldn't say they are bigger than the Beatles – because they had a fantastic career – they are just doing things faster."

The band's tour manager had told them it would take three years of "hard graft" to do well in America. But he had underestimated the power of social media.

"For it to have taken off as it has is incredible," Liam told a reporter from the *Daily Mirror* who had flown out to New York. "Twitter has been a major factor in getting our name out there in the States. Just as Twitter has gone up, so we have, too. They've gone hand in hand. And, picture-wise, Tumblr has helped us a lot. It has really accelerated our success."

Niall also underlined the importance of social media. "It's the main thing that we're about," he told a broadcaster. "If you ask fans where they found out about us it's always Twitter, YouTube, Tumblr, Facebook. It's the most powerful thing we have."

The boys' hands-on personal involvement was crucial to their success. While some pop stars or actors let management employees handle their social media news and messages to fans, the One Direction boys always posted their own.

"It's really important that we connect directly with our fans through the likes of Twitter so they can get to know us," explained Harry. "There would be no point someone in the office doing it because that would defeat the object. We kept in contact with them and gave them something to look forward to."

Harry told an American reporter, "Whenever we talk to people from the label back home they don't know what's going on – everyone's just overwhelmed by the reaction. We're just loving it." He said his band's achievement was "incredibly humbling".

Zayn played down the many comparisons with the Beatles. "It seems ridiculous for that sort of thing to apply to you – you laugh about it, someone comparing you to such a huge phenomenon."

★   ★   ★

After a brief return to the UK, the boys were back in the States again. One particularly big night for them was at Nickelodeon's 25th annual Kids' Choice Awards in LA, hosted by Will Smith, where the winners received an orange-coloured blimp trophy.

Taylor Swift received a special silver-coloured Big Help Award blimp from First Lady Michelle Obama, for her efforts in assisting American tornado and flood survivors. As One Direction performed 'What Makes You Beautiful', Taylor joined Selena Gomez in an ostentatious display of dancing at the front of the stage. It seemed designed to get her noticed, and it worked.

Later, Taylor got chatting to Justin Bieber, confiding in him that she fancied Harry. Justin joked that he was trying to keep his own girlfriend, Selena Gomez, away from the band because she too loved them.

Taylor Swift hung around the boys' dressing room and said a quick hello to them. Then, according to one source, she started dramatically fanning herself with one hand to indicate how overcome she was at meeting them up close. They all laughed but she had cleverly made her feelings felt, with frequent glances at Harry. He had noticed her dancing earlier and later mentioned it on Twitter.

The boys met Michelle Obama backstage and she invited them to the White House for the annual Easter egg hunt on Easter Monday. Unfortunately, they were unable to attend because they would be off on a tour of Australia.

Meanwhile, Demi Lovato, who Niall admitted he had a crush on, returned the compliment during a promotional tour in Europe for her latest album, *Unbroken*. Asked in a web chat with MSN Music who she found hot in the showbiz world, Demi, 19, named Niall: "He's so adorable."

Niall had fallen for Demi after watching an MTV documentary on her, called *Stay Strong*, earlier in the year, which followed her personal struggles, including a stay in rehab for eating disorders and drinking problems. Niall described it as an "amazing story".

While in the US, One Direction heard some more incredible news from their management company. Just six weeks earlier, they had arrived in America as the support act for Big Time Rush. Now they were booked to headline New York's world-renowned Madison Square Garden in December.

While rehearsing in New York for their performance on the *Saturday Night Live* TV show, they bumped into Justin Bieber, who happened to be recording in the same studio. He invited them to listen to some tracks from his new album and later told them they should "hook up" again to work on new material together.

Harry thought the attractive guest host of *Saturday Night Live*, 39-year-old Sofia Vergara, was "hot". She was in the dressing room opposite the boys and they left the door open quite a bit, so that Harry could get a good peek at her.

On the show they wore curly wigs and bushy moustaches in a comedy sketch that had them playing the members of a Mexican band – called Juan Direction. They were given Mexican names: Harry was Carlito, Louis was Pepito, Liam was Matito, Zayn was Miguelito, and Niall was, bizarrely, called Dick!

As well as starring in the sketch, they also performed their hits, 'What Makes You Beautiful' and 'One Thing'. It was a polished, almost relaxed live performance and they looked like they were really enjoying themselves. The boys later agreed that it was one of their favourite appearances to date.

While doing some promos for Nickelodeon, Louis and Zayn were in on a prank that worked spectacularly well when Harry, Niall and Liam fell for it completely:

An actress is playing a producer and has a large prosthetic bump under her top, to give the impression she is heavily pregnant. She sits down with them and tells how the baby is "kicking her bladder", asking if they would like to sing to the baby to calm it down. The boys start singing 'Rock-a-bye-Baby'!

Suddenly she cries, "The baby is coming!" and screams with pain. She gets Harry to hold her from behind as she squats. Then she asks to be laid on the floor. Harry, in particular, starts to panic, asking, "Why is no one here?" Not wanting to leave her side, he asks Niall to find someone but, oddly, Niall has his hands in his pockets, looking totally clueless and unfazed! Liam calls out, "Can somebody help us?"

Liam initially tries to make the woman comfortable. She asks him to call her husband to tell him his baby is on the way. Taking the phone he tells him, "We're with your wife and she's in a lot of pain. We know she's pregnant and she might be giving birth."

Meanwhile, Harry holds her hands and joins in her pain-relieving breathing exercises! Amid the panic, Louis complains of a strange smell and the actress confesses, "I'm sorry. I farted. I'm pregnant." They start giggling but then, as her moans and groans increase, they look horrified. It's at that moment that she puts them out of their misery by telling them, "You've been pranked by Nickelodeon!"

Niall and Liam are visibly shocked, while Louis and Zayn laugh, high-five and hug each other. But it's all a bit much for an incredulous Harry, who falls to the floor and then has to be consoled by the actress. "Harry was the worst! You were so embarrassing!" Louis teases.

Later, Harry remarked, "I was actually thinking, 'This is going to be a great press story. One Direction deliver a child.'"

★ ★ ★

On April 9, 2012, they touched down in Sydney for the start of their Australasian promotional tour. It followed a tried and tested pattern in that they would later return to play a series of gigs. Hundreds of fans had camped outside the airport hoping for a glimpse of them, but they were bitterly disappointed to be informed that the 'Fab Five' had been whisked through a back door.

Later, Zayn delighted his fans by posing at the window of his hotel room, shirtless and showing off a heart tattoo on his stomach.

In Sydney Harbour, the boys relaxed on a private yacht prior to kicking off their tour. Here they lapped up the sunshine and enjoyed a beer. During their first week they performed at Australia's *Logie Awards*, celebrating the TV industry, and also appeared on breakfast TV show *Sunrise*, where a noisy crowd gathered outside the studio. A huge monitor outside showed the band being interviewed, and each time there was a close-up of one of them, screams and cheers rang out.

When they arrived to do an interview on Sydney's Nova radio station, Harry asked the show's host, Ryan 'Fitzy' Fitzgerald, the name of the girl on the front desk. Told it was Anna [Crotti], he dreamily replied, "She's lovely." Zayn chipped in, "She's hot." When Harry was asked by Fitzy what he wanted to do in Australia, he looked at the show's co-host, Michael 'Wippa' Wipfli, and mouthed, "Anna."

Their comments were trending on Twitter overnight. By the following day, Anna was big news and was interviewed on the radio show. She had a lot to say:

"I didn't know what had been said. Then their security guard came out – and I thought I was in trouble – but he said, 'The boys want your number.' I wrote it on a Post-It note and gave it to him and didn't really think about it. Later I got a text message from Zayn which just said, 'Hey babe.' I had an idea who it was but I texted back, 'Hey. Who is this? Sorry, I don't have this number saved on my phone.' He texted, 'Ha ha. I just took your number at the radio station. Zayn.' I replied, 'Hi Zayn. How's your day going? Anna.' He replied, 'OK.'"

Anna laughed at the recollection, saying that he appeared a bit unimpressed by her coolness. She went on: "I texted, 'Sorry, this is all a bit weird for me. But it was good to meet you.' He replied, 'Yeah, it was good to meet you too. Are you busy tonight?'

"He wanted to go for drinks and later back to his hotel – but only because anywhere else there would be cameras and people and all this other stuff."

When asked by Wippa if there were any 'Xs' at the end of his text messages, Anna replied: "There were Xs all over the place. And smiley faces. I didn't go to the hotel because by the end of the day it got so intense. I quickly checked Facebook before I left and I was getting random girls adding me on Facebook. I got some girls calling the radio station, giving me a little bit of shit. I didn't even want to walk home. It was so intense.

"I messaged Zayn and said maybe it's not a good idea we meet up. It was just a bit too full-on."

Anna, who has been in a relationship for two years, was rattled by some of the hostility she received from One Direction fans. "I know it's just typical teenage girl stuff but I don't understand it," she said.

★   ★   ★

Liam took the opportunity to go surfing in Australia, and took Louis along with him to Manly Beach in Sydney one morning, leaving the other three to do yet more radio interviews. As Zayn told an interviewer on radio station Sea 90.9 who asked what his greatest fear was, he was frightened of water because he couldn't swim.

All of them visited a casino and most made heavy losses – apart from Niall, who won $100 and stopped while he was ahead. But he was alarmed by the others and tried to stop them continuing to lose money. They seemed hooked and it took some persuading before they eventually walked away.

While they were in Australia, a Californian band launched a lawsuit against them – claiming they were the first to be called One Direction, having formed in 2009. They said they had recorded two albums and had a significant following in the US, and had filed a trademark application for the use of the name 'One Direction' with the US Patent and Trademark Office in February 2011.

They wanted a share of the profits earned by the British boys and demanded more than $1 million in damages. Harry, Liam, Niall, Louis and Zayn were named, along with Syco and Sony Music Entertainment, in the lawsuit.

Meanwhile, over in the US, Justin Bieber teasingly let slip that "one of the world's biggest artists" fancied Harry Styles. Talking to reporters, he said of One Direction, "They look great, they sound great and, when you add their British accents into the mix, the American girls are going crazy for them. I already know one of the biggest artists in the world thinks Harry is so hot, but I have been sworn to secrecy."

It was no secret to Harry's bandmates though. He and Taylor Swift, 22, had exchanged a string of text messages while they were in Australia. Things were definitely hotting up between them.

Bizarrely, the boys found themselves at the centre of very different speculation after they cuddled koala bears at a sanctuary in Brisbane. They were told that up to 80 per cent of koalas in Australia are infected with the sexual disease chlamydia, and that they may have been infected by contact with them – particularly after one urinated on Liam!

A stunned Liam commented: "I'm genuinely scared. This is worrying. I'd have never picked the thing up if I'd known." Fortunately, the boys were given the all-clear and Liam and Louis were spared having to try to explain how they picked up the disease to their girlfriends back home!

When they moved on to New Zealand, Liam was taken aback to be asked by a TV reporter if he was a good lover. He replied, "Louis and I both have girlfriends, so we must be doing something right. I've had my girlfriend for a long time, so I'm definitely doing something right."

More musically relevant, during a chat on the radio station *Newstalk* in Auckland, Harry dismissed comparisons with the 'Fab Four' when the host said he hadn't seen "a fever like this since the Beatles".

"Whenever somebody brings up the Beatles, it's always something we kind of dismiss because they are a whole another level," Harry said. "In our opinion they are the biggest boy band that will ever be. So for us to get that kind of comparison is ridiculous. But obviously very flattering at the same time."

Harry also talked about how fortuitous it was that all of their parents had got to know each other and kept in contact when their sons were abroad. "As we go through things together, we have each other to talk to," he explained. "And while we're away from home it's nice for our parents to be in touch with each other because they are going through the same thing. If my mum doesn't know what's going on, it's nice for her to be able to speak to Niall's mum and say, 'Do you know what they are doing?'"

In Auckland, Liam and Louis – who paired up a lot in Australasia – made a bungee jump from the top of the 192-metre Sky Tower. Later, they joined the rest of the group to watch the Australia v New Zealand rugby league match.

As for Harry, when he wasn't texting Taylor Swift he was enjoying the company of Victoria's Secret model Emma Ostilly, 18. She had been sharing a house in Auckland since moving there from America, but, when news got out, she was the latest in the line to receive jealous abuse on Twitter.

A few days before they were due to fly home to Britain, Niall was hit by food poisoning and felt very sick on the plane back. When he got home, he soothed his tummy with what he called the "Irish remedy" – flat 7 Up.

The boys welcomed a two-week rest and the chance to get back to a semblance of normal life, after the fan mania in Australasia and America. Liam and Louis were also pleased to be back with their girlfriends.

Harry drove back to Cheshire in his new Audi R8 to see his family, and later met up with former childhood sweetheart Fliss Skinner, taking her out to dinner at the restaurant Gusto in Alderley Edge.

He also let his old White Eskimo pal, Nick Clough, have a drive. Nick thought it was "amazing", and later described: "Everyone in the houses on my estate was at their windows. We had a little drive around, catching up, listening to music. He had a CD in the car that Caroline Flack made for him. It was made up of cute little songs that they listened to together. One song on there was 'Call Me Maybe' and we were singing along to it. Then we went to McDonald's and had a drive-through."

Zayn was back with Little Mix singer Perrie Edwards, and they went to the cinema to see *Avengers Assemble*. But Perrie was not happy about his flirtatious texts to Anna Crotti in Australia, and Zayn had his work cut out getting back into her good books. Perrie was not in the best of moods and told him she thought the film was "boring".

Having dined out a lot on his travels, Louis enjoyed the simple pleasure of eating one of his favourite snacks – fish finger sandwiches – which girlfriend Eleanor Calder made him in her student flat in Manchester. Many of his former school pals were now at university and Louis enjoyed a taste of student life with Eleanor.

While back in Doncaster, Louis met up with his pal Stan and they took part in an Aston Martin race day. They also attended the big football match in Manchester as City took on United; Louis was disappointed with the result though, as United lost one-nil.

Niall went to watch horse racing at Kilbeggan in Westmeath, and enjoyed a beer or two with friends. An onlooker said: "He was very low-key but was happy to sign autographs and pose with fans. He seemed to enjoy himself."

While back in Mullingar, Niall hooked up with a female friend, 17-year-old Ali McGinley, who he had got to know before flying out to the US. Now back in town, he called her up and they went out to a nightclub together, as well as to a bowling alley.

Niall confirmed his love of Ireland in his own unique way in an interview with *Fabulous* magazine: "One hundred per cent Ireland is my home. When I get off the plane and it smells like cow poo and pints of Guinness, I know I'm home."

Harry spent a night out with pretty actress Emily Atack, 22, from hit TV comedy series *Inbetweeners*, who had fancied Harry for some time. Meanwhile, Caroline Flack got hot and bothered when she appeared on British comedian Leigh Francis' panel show, *Celebrity Juice*.

Francis was appearing in the guise of his alter ego, outspoken presenter Keith Lemon. Introducing the celebrity panellists, he archly asked what Caroline had been up to recently. There were giggles in the studio as she smiled and nonchalantly replied, "Oh, you know. Hanging out."

"*X Factor*," said Keith. "Are you doing another one?" Caroline started to reply about the possibility of a further series of *Xtra Factor*, when the sniggers amongst fellow panellists and the audience made her aware of his innuendo.

"I'm doing... um..." she stammered but Keith, enjoying the moment, quickly interjected, "Caroline, what *direction* do you see you career going?"

"I don't know," she replied, now going red and fanning herself with her hand.

"What sort of music are you listening to these days? The Wanted? Take That? What about One Direction?" asked Keith.

"Yeah, they're good," she replied, still smiling and going even redder.

"Which member would you say was your favourite one? That fellow with the hair is good, isn't he?" As a picture of Harry appeared on the screen, Caroline replied, "He's all right."

Then the eternally juvenile Keith went for the jugular: "When you were having sex with him, did he just giggle at your boobs?"

As everyone roared with laughter, Caroline protested, "Oh my God! Too far!"

★  ★  ★

In May 2012, One Direction were back in Stockholm to start work on the second album. While they were waving to a screaming crowd of fans from a balcony, some of the girls flashed their breasts at them. Zayn was so shocked that he held his hand to his face and turned away!

But it was something that they had to get used to while in Sweden, because the breast flashing happened on several occasions. Intriguingly, it hadn't happened anywhere else!

On another occasion they were in their car when a girl ran up, lifted her top and pressed her bare breast against the window. Once they had got over the shock, they laughed to see that an imprint had been left behind!

Sweden was also notable for having one of the most determined – and patient – fans. A girl hid in a bin outside their hotel for four hours, hoping to gain access to the hotel through the back entrance. But she was discovered by security staff, who were astonished when she told them she had been hiding in the cramped, smelly bin for such a long time.

By the end of the month, One Direction were back in the US for a major North American Tour which would follow through to July. No longer a support act, they were now major headliners, landing at Logan Airport in Boston to the by-now habitual screams from the gathered crowd.

President Obama's 14-year-old daughter, Malia, was amongst the packed crowd at the Patriot Centre in Fairfax, Virginia, on the opening night of the tour, just three rows back from the stage. As the almost exclusively teenaged female audience stood up and sang along to the songs, a rather embarrassed looking secret service agent tried to hide himself in the seat behind her.

One Direction were, of course, used to screaming fans. A few days later, however, they were genuinely shaken while strolling through Manhattan on a day off when a large group of fans mobbed them, pulling at their hair and clothes in their eagerness to make contact. Liam and Niall later tweeted about the incident and they were still clearly ruffled. "This is a complete joke. Ridic. Day off, wanna chill," wrote Niall. Even the usually composed Liam was upset, writing, "That wasn't even funny."

The gigs played to capacity audiences, and a popular part of each one was a Twitter Q&A session with the audience halfway through. Once more it served to bond the band with their fans, who loved to hear about their likes and dislikes, their funny stories – in fact, any scrap of information about them at all.

Some eager fans checked into the same hotel as them in order to get closer; others just hung around in the lobby and Harry was startled when some girls took video footage of him working out in the gym.

With Harry and Zayn getting more and more tattoos, Niall decided he was going to have 'Made In Ireland' tattooed on his backside. He went with the others to a tattoo parlour in LA, but they refused to do it. Niall's colleagues fell about laughing when the tattooist explained that the skin on Niall's backside wasn't tight enough!

Eleanor Calder joined Louis in New York. Later, when they moved on to Canada, she was with the boys when they visited Niagara Falls.

Here they took a ride on the Maid of the Mist boat, wearing plastic rain covers to protect them from the falls' spray. They later stopped to buy a snack at Taco Bell and enjoyed close-up descents into the gorge of the falls as well as the Bird Kingdom – the world's largest, free-flying, indoor aviary, featuring over 500 colourful birds.

When attention from some fans got too much, the boys had to be escorted away in a police car to a nearby arcade. One misguided girl wasn't giving up and got herself arrested after she tried to break into the car.

The boys' pal, Olly Murs, flew out to join them as a guest artist on stage in Toronto at the Molson Amphitheatre, where he opened the show. He had the girls screaming when he informed them that Niall told him the Toronto fans were his favourites.

When they played in Mexico City, Harry noticed mid-song that a small girl was being crushed in the front row by fans trying to get closer to the stage. He stopped singing and bent down to a security guard, pointing to the girl, as the others continued with the song. Standing back up, Harry joined in with the singing once more but then stopped again to point to the girl. When the security guard eventually lifted her over the barrier, Harry looked relieved, smiled and gave him the thumbs up.

Back in the States, fiery celebrity chef Gordon Ramsay invited the boys to his steak restaurant in Las Vegas. Niall described him as a "top dog".

In Houston, a fan was dressed like Louis' girlfriend, Eleanor, outside the hotel where the boys were staying. She wore the same outfit that Eleanor had previously worn and her hair was styled the same way. She was telling everyone that she *was* Eleanor Calder and posed for pictures with fans. Louis saw her and even *he* thought she looked like his girlfriend!

Onstage in Houston, Niall had to take prompt action to prevent serious injury. A fan had thrown an iPhone at him, to which she had Sellotaped house keys and a sexually suggestive note. He only saw it coming at the last moment, quickly slapping it down before it hit him in the face.

Another fan, in Anaheim, California, had a much better way of getting their attention. After One Direction sang their last number, she threw a walkie-talkie onstage. Harry noticed it and picked it up; the girl had kept hold of the other one and he chatted to her through it!

During a break, the boys went fishing on a boat off the coast of San Diego and Liam was startled to find he'd hooked a baby tiger shark. It was thrown back in the water, but he was proud to have landed it on only his second ever fishing trip.

On the *Entertainment Tonight* show, Liam told the interviewer what all their personality traits were: "Louis is the joker of the band, Niall the cute Irish one, Zayn is the quiet mysterious man and Harry is the curly guy who is very cheeky and likes women." After a pause, he clarified, "We *all* like women," and Louis added, "Liam's the daddy."

The boys had been thoroughly enjoying their tour, but there was one thing that Niall was desperately missing – beer! Back home he was old enough to drink alcohol – but not in America, where the legal drinking age in most States was 21.

"I'm an Irishman. I like a pint!" he complained to the others.

Florida was their last stop on the tour. On radio station 93.3 FLZ, the interviewer read out a cheeky question from a fan, asking if they slept 'commando'. They did. All of them – but, naturally, it was Harry, who expressed it: "Let it all hang out."

While in Florida, they took the opportunity to visit Universal Islands of Adventure in Orlando. With Olly Murs in tow, they tried out a new attraction called Despicable Me Minion Mayhem, along with the Hulk rollercoaster ride and the Wizarding World of Harry Potter. Louis described it as one of his best days in America, and Liam – who had been on holiday to Florida with his family as a youngster – called the State his "favourite place in the world".

Harry was the only one of the band who didn't go. He was not in the best of moods and wanted to keep a low profile. As they prepared to fly back home after a hugely successful tour, he knew he was entering

131

into a storm after having heard that his affair with DJ Lucy Horobin had become public. And the fact that she was newly married at the time was the sort of publicity Harry did not need.

# 11

# Going Global

Back home in July, it was Niall who got into trouble when he arrived at Dublin Airport. As a small group of teenage girls called his name, he turned and called them a "shower of c★★★s".

The remark shocked many people once the footage was shown on YouTube. Yet the girls themselves had not taken offence, in fact they were pleased when he had said, "Happy birthday" to one of them when asked to. Amazingly, one of the girls also apologised to Niall for getting him into trouble.

While it's true that Niall – like many of his fellow countrymen – uses swear words liberally and usually in a good-humoured way, with no offence meant or taken, this incident was, at the very least, misjudged. He was quick to apologise via Twitter: "Really sorry if I caused any offence. It was just banter with fans who I think of more as mates but I understand that it's not a word I should be using at all."

Meanwhile, as Harry's affair with Lucy Horobin had been all over the papers, he remained silent on the subject and started dating reality TV star Caggie Dunlop, 23, who appears in the British TV series *Made In Chelsea*. The pair had got to know each other the previous summer, having met at a party, and had kept in touch.

But later in the year, the affair with Lucy Horobin was to hit the newspapers again when her husband, Oliver Pope, spoke to the *Daily Mirror* about it just days before he was due to file for divorce. Oliver, 31, revealed that Lucy had told him she no longer loved him, just three days before bedding Harry.

"The moment I discovered Harry had slept with my wife still haunts me," he said. "Knowing they slept together and then Lucy came back home and climbed into bed with me hurts the most.

"Realising my wife had decided to leave me because she had fallen for a 17-year-old boy, that's the most embarrassing thing."

He added, "I know how stupid it sounds but I blame Harry 100 per cent for this. OK, so Lucy may have technically split from me days before he first slept with her but that came after weeks of flirtatious text messages. We were still living together in the same house. At that point, in the same bed. She was wearing a wedding ring the first time they met."

Oliver told how the cracks began in their marriage after the first time Lucy met Harry and the boys, interviewing them on her radio show. It was, he believed, the precursor to her telling Oliver she no longer loved him.

★ ★ ★

Just a few days after returning home, Niall was flying out once more – this time on a holiday to Marbella with his dad, Bobby, and some pals from Mullingar. While he was there, he started flirting with a fellow Brit, 26-year-old estate agent Ruth Hicks, who was with a hen party.

When a picture of the pair appeared together, as she enjoyed a cocktail at a pool party at the Ocean Club, Ruth became the next in the firing line for jealous fans. But she insisted their jealousy was misplaced, because she wasn't romantically interested in him at all – although *he* was in her.

As she told the *Irish Sun*: "We only spent about 15 minutes in each other's company, and we didn't kiss. Niall seemed like a sweet boy and I think he fancied his chances with me. He was very flirty. But I told him I was engaged and he moved on. He's not my type anyway – he's too young, too puny and too short. And I am very much in love with my fiancé."

Liam was soon flying away again, this time for a romantic break in Venice with Danielle, where they enjoyed a gondola ride. They also visited St Mark's Square, where they took a look around the ornate basilica.

But things were less idyllic when he returned home to the UK, where some fans knocked on his door in the middle of the night. He later tweeted: "I just wanna say I love you guys and all but having strangers knock on my door and notes pushed through at 11 p.m. can be a little bit scary."

When Harry returned to Cheshire, he was mobbed by a group of teenage fans outside his family home. His Range Rover was surrounded by around 20 girls clamouring to meet him. Worried about driving into them, he got out and walked the short distance to his mother's house.

That July, Harry, Liam and Niall all attended the wedding of JLS singer Marvin Humes to Rochelle Wiseman of the Saturdays, at Blenheim Palace in Oxfordshire. Then it was back to recording, to finish the album.

Ed Sheeran had written a couple of songs – 'Little Things' and 'Over Again' for their second album, *Take Me Home*, which was to be released in the UK in November. The boys recorded the tracks in a studio in Buckinghamshire; afterwards, as they drove back to London with Ed, Harry felt the urge to shed some clothes once more. The others were by now getting used to such antics, but Ed was startled.

"I turned around and Harry was stripped off completely naked, just sitting there laughing," he told Australia's 2Day FM. "Literally, I was just looking out the window, watching cars going past. I turn around, all the boys are kind of shocked and there's just him laughing, completely naked."

Simon Cowell also popped into the studio to hear some of the new songs on the album. Although he had an easygoing relationship with them, now that they were no longer in *The X Factor*, the boys still felt a familiar tingling of nerves when they sang new material to him, wondering whether he would like it or not. As Liam commented, "Some things never change."

A few days after returning to London, Harry had a date with Burberry model Cara Delevingne at one of Soho's private members' clubs, Omega House. They had been on a date earlier in the summer at Mayfair nightclub Le Baron, and had kept in touch via text.

Meanwhile, Liam went for one of his routine medical check-ups and was surprised and delighted to be told that both of his kidneys were now working fine. Niall joked with the near teetotal singer that it was time to get him down the pub for a pint!

A couple of days later, on August 12, the band took part in the closing ceremony of the 2012 London Olympics. They sang 'What Makes You Beautiful' to a packed venue and millions watching around the world.

The Spice Girls had also got back together to perform. Afterwards, One Direction got to meet them backstage and Liam made a bit of a fool of himself with Victoria Beckham. He happily kissed Geri, Mel B, Mel C and Emma, but, worried about Victoria's rather stern demeanour, he awkwardly held back from kissing her. Then he changed his mind and quickly leaned forward for a peck on both cheeks, but she pulled away after the first kiss, looking a bit shocked. Louis, standing nearby, had a good laugh at Liam's uncomfortable moment!

Harry texted his stepdad, Robin, to tell him that he was mingling with the likes of Brian May and Pete Townshend in the backstage VIP area. Rock fan Robin was suitably impressed. He had also been stunned when, on an earlier occasion, Harry had met Rolling Stone Ronnie Wood, who joked that he wanted to come and play the guitar with One Direction.

Liam celebrated his 19th birthday on August 29, 2012, at the Funky Buddha club in London's Mayfair, with all of the band apart from Zayn – who stayed at home to watch his girlfriend, Perrie Edwards, perform on TV game show *Red Or Black* with her band, Little Mix. Liam, who was accompanied by Danielle Peazer, was all smiles as he received a Batman-themed birthday cake.

Niall celebrated his own 19th birthday two weeks later back home in Mullingar, where he was the star at Keith Duffy's annual golf fundraiser for autism. He had spent the morning visiting homeless shelters in Mullingar before taking part in the tournament. Hundreds of excited fans had arrived after they had heard he was taking part, and some had been there since the crack of dawn.

Niall's mother, Maura, his stepfather, Chris, father, Bobby, and brother Greg were also present. "We don't get to see enough of him," Maura told the newspapers. "We try and steal a minute with him every chance we get."

Keith Duffy had not realised that it was Niall Horan who had caddied for him as a young lad four years earlier. When Niall arrived and saw Keith, her shouted, "Oi Duffy. You don't remember me, do ya?"

A puzzled Keith asked how he might know him outside of One Direction and Niall replied, "I was the gobshite who took yer clubs out of yer BMW. I caddied for you."

Keith laughed and said, "Oh! you were the cheeky yob who caddied for me?" And Niall had him laughing even harder when he replied, "That was me. You gave me 50 euros, you tight git!'"

Niall was looking forward to meeting his celebrity crush, Demi Lovato, at the MTV Video Music Awards a few days later. They had never met but had become text and Twitter pals. Demi had previously denied reports she was dating Niall, insisting, "He's really sweet and he's one of my really good friends now. But I'm single at the moment and I plan to be for a long time because I need to focus on my career, myself and my well-being." None of which apparently allowed any place for Niall.

In an informal but televised chat backstage on *The X Factor USA*, judge Demi Lovato said to Simon Cowell, "By the way, Niall says hi."

"Oh, what, from One Direction?" Simon replied. "Keep away from him. He's pure."

She laughed and said, "Excuse me? I'm not looking for anything."

"Really?" Simon teased.

Demi insisted, "Yes, I'm not going to date anybody for a whole year." She added that she had "made that clear" to Niall.

Simon then asked her if she had kissed Niall; she laughed and insisted, "No!"

A chuckling Simon ended by assuring her, "Don't worry. This will never be seen… much."

As Liam was to tell *Top Of The Pops* magazine: "Niall understands girls the least because he hasn't got any sisters. You generally understand girls a little more if you've grown up around them."

Meanwhile, the US band who had called themselves One Direction dropped their lawsuit after an undisclosed deal was made. They agreed to be renamed Uncharted Shores.

Further good news came a few days later at the MTV Video Music Awards, held at the Staples Center in Los Angeles, where One Direction were the biggest success of the evening. They were up for three awards: Best New Artist, Best Pop Video and the oddly titled Most Share-Worthy Video – the last two for 'What Makes You Beautiful'. To their delight, they won all three categories and each got a kiss from Katy Perry when she presented them with one of the awards. She was yet another of Niall's celebrity crushes and afterwards he stammered, "Wow, thank you very much Katy. Thanks for the kiss. Thank you so much."

He also found time to chat with Demi Lovato, who won the award for Best Video With A Message with 'Skyscraper'. The pair talked animatedly for some time. "They seemed like old friends and were very relaxed in each other's company," said a fellow guest. "Niall was doing most of the talking and he made her laugh a lot. They looked like they were getting on very well together."

One Direction sang 'One Thing' and had the crowd screaming and dancing. It was to become another of their favourite performances. Back home, Harry's mum, Anne, stayed up until 3 a.m. watching the show on TV and was in tears of joy by the end. She was immensely proud of her boy and had become very fond of all of the boys in the band.

After the show, they headed for Justin Bieber's house for a party. They were still heady from the excitement and their success at the awards, but were surprised when Justin headed for the kitchen to partake in the not-so-rock'n'roll activity of cooking noodles. But Niall good-naturedly helped out.

Still on a high, Niall later tweeted Katy Perry a picture of them kissing on stage, with the caption "looks like its official… me and you". In a reference to the famous movie *The Graduate*, about an older woman who seduces a college student, Katy pinged back the flirtatious reply, "I'll be your Mrs Robinson."

Louis and Liam got into the swim of things during some downtime in Florida. Louis visited the Miami Seaquarium with Eleanor, where he donned a wetsuit to go swimming with a dolphin. First off, a trainer told him about dolphin physiology and behaviour, followed by 30 minutes in the water where he got to share 'handshakes', rubs, feeding techniques and kisses! The highlight was holding on to the dolphin's dorsal as it pulled him through the water.

Later, he wore a scuba diving helmet for a 20-minute underwater journey through a 300,000-gallon simulated tropical reef, where he encountered colourful tropical fish, stingrays and a variety of unique sea creatures. Along with other divers, he also got to feed schools of fish and rays. 'Showtime' was provided by a killer whale and white-sided dolphins leapt gracefully out of the water at a trainer's command.

Liam made a splash at SeaWorld in Orlando, where he too got in amongst the dolphins and went face to face behind a glass wall with a killer whale. He was enjoying a family holiday which also saw a visit to Disneyworld, where he had his picture taken with Mickey Mouse. After riding on the stomach-churning Space Mountain and Splash Mountain rides, Liam headed over to the nearby Hollywood Studios for a spine-chilling ride on the elevator of the Tower of Terror, which he later said was "amazing!"

Later that month, Harry Styles was seen prominently in the front row at London Fashion Week, commencing September 17, 2012, as Cara Delevingne sashayed down the catwalk.

Meanwhile, Emma Watson had heard from Harry's Radio 1 DJ pal, Nick Grimshaw, after she was a guest on his breakfast show, that Harry had left halfway through a special screening of her latest film, *The Perks Of Being A Wallflower*. Afterwards, she took to Twitter to teasingly ask him when he was going to see the second half of her movie. When he was later asked by a newspaper why he hadn't answered Emma's message, Harry said that he'd failed to notice it among his daily avalanche of tweets and that he'd find it.

A few days later he replied to Emma's tweet, telling her that he had to leave to go back to work. He added, "I heard the second half is very good and I will be going to see it again." Desperately trying to compensate for what seemed like a slight, he later tweeted, "hiiii... I'm going to watch it now. On the up side, it was the best first half of a film I've ever seen... "

It took him four months before he watched the movie in full, and he eventually tweeted Emma again to say, "I finally saw the second half! That film gets dark, but I liked it a lot." Emma replied, "yay!! So happy."

★   ★   ★

Having performed around the world, the boys enjoyed giving a concert at the iTunes Festival at the Roundhouse, in Camden, north London, where they sang a string of their hits to the familiar screams from fans. "We've spent a lot of time away and I just wanted to say how incredible it is to be back in London," Louis called from the stage. But the level of noise from their performances was starting to affect his hearing.

As he told the *Daily Mirror*: "I am going slightly deaf in my right ear. It's tinnitus... something like that. All our fans are always very loud."

Meanwhile, Zayn's relationship with Perrie Edwards was progressing to the point where she had invited him to meet her family in Newcastle. Zayn was a bit worried about what her muscular navy recruit brother thought of him, but in the event they got on well.

However, Liam's romance with Danielle Peazer came to an end in September, after two years together. Louis' girlfriend, Eleanor, had frequently flown out to be with him on his travels, but Danielle had not done so with Liam. The long periods spent apart had put a strain on their relationship and they'd eventually decided to call time.

A few days later, Harry was reunited with Taylor Swift at BBC Radio 1's Teen Awards, which were held at Wembley Arena in northwest London. One Direction were once more the big award winner with Best Single, Best Album and Best Music Act. They sent the fans wild as they performed on a floating plinth above their heads, while Taylor also sang on the night, wearing tight silver shorts that showed off her long legs. She and Harry got deep into conversation backstage and a proper romance was to develop.

Their latest single, 'Live While We're Young', was released at the end of September and shot to the top of the US charts, meanwhile reaching number three in the UK. While shooting the video for it at Eridge Park Estate in the Kent countryside, Louis once more showed that he was a liability in a car. The video sees them waking up in a tent in a field, swinging on ropes into a stream and then jumping into a jeep for a ride along a bumpy track. Louis is at the wheel and, even in the edited video, you can see the others almost falling out of their seats as the jeep speeds along the uneven terrain.

"He was driving like an absolute nutter," Liam told British morning TV show *Daybreak*. "When we went over a bump the back kind of came off the vehicle."

In mid-October, the boys returned to Dublin for their second appearance on *The Late Late Show*. After arriving the night before, they enjoyed hitting the local pubs and clubs with Niall acting as their very own guide.

Harry, Louis and Liam also had some tattoos done: Harry had the words 'Things I Can' etched on the inside of one arm, and 'Things I Can't' written on the inside of the other; Louis and Liam both had screws drawn on their ankles.

Louis became managing director of his former pub football team in Doncaster, the Three Horse Shoes. He set up a fixture with a team from Doncaster Rovers at the Keepmoat Stadium, which the Horse Shoes won 2-1 – and as MD, Louis made sure he played! The new strip he bought the team was sponsored by Yorkshire Tea – Louis' favourite. Harry, Niall and Liam were there to cheer him on at the match in aid of charity, and the money went to a local children's hospice, Bluebell Wood in Sheffield, of which Louis is a patron.

The boys further showed their charitable side when they met with some young medical patients at a London hotel. The occasion was organised by Rays Of Sunshine, which seeks to grant the wishes of seriously (or terminally) ill children. The boys are all ambassadors of the charity and they were clearly touched by the youngsters they met. As Liam commented: "We really love doing things like this. We leave smiling because they are always so wonderful."

When a three-year-old girl with heart problems complained that she was hungry, Liam went off to find her some biscuits. And a cheeky seven-year-old girl named Niamh, who was recovering from burns, had Harry laughing when she handed him a poster she made with newspaper headlines which referred to his romance with Caroline Flack. One read, "Caroline In Bits When Dumped", and another "Gutted Over Harry's Secret Love For Niamh". She wagged her finger at Harry, saying, "Now are you going to behave? This was when you were being very naughty," as he protested his innocence.

As Niall said: "It is totally humbling to meet kids like this. And it really makes you feel good that you can do something nice for them. We've had amazing good luck and many of these children haven't. But they are always happy and we go away feeling brilliant. It's like we're giving something back."

One Direction's management team showed its usual flair for immaculate timing when the boys went on a short promo tour of Europe, just prior to the release of *Take Me Home*. Flying out on a private jet to Madrid on October 31, 2012, before going on to Milan and Stockholm, they gave several press conferences and TV and radio interviews, as well as appearing on the Italian and Swedish versions of *The X Factor*.

At a press conference in Milan, Harry spoke once more about the influence that social media had played in promoting them around the world. "We are very lucky to have such a strong following on things like Twitter and Facebook," he said. "When we were younger we didn't have that way of being able to get close to our favourite bands. For us it's very important in terms of keeping a close relationship with our fans and to let them know what we are doing."

Many German fans got excited when Harry revealed, on *The Dome* TV show, that he had an uncle and a cousin who lived in Hamburg.

Meanwhile, Louis had been taking 'souvenirs' home with him of each country he visited. But 'taking' was the key word. If he saw something he wanted, he just took it without paying for it. At the hotel in Stockholm where they were staying, there was a stuffed goose in a display cabinet which he liked and so he simply took it. Louis called the goose 'Gerald', and it ended up in the house of his girlfriend, Eleanor's, parents.

★    ★    ★

*Take Me Home* was released mid-November 2012. Not only did One Direction share some of the writing credits on five of the tracks, but Niall got to play guitar – to the envy of Louis, who harboured ambitions to play a guitar himself.

For two weeks, as they completed the album in London, they had existed mostly on fast food brought in from nearby Thai and Portuguese restaurants. They spent so long holed up inside the recording studio that they joked about getting "studio tan" – a deathly shade of green!

They also went a little stir crazy. Although there were fans constantly outside, the band were not allowed out to meet them as it was considered a security risk. But Louis and Zayn crept up onto the roof and looked over the edge, until furious security staff shouted at them to come down.

As the money came rolling in from their astonishing worldwide success, Liam prickled at criticism from those who suggested that they were not worthy of such rewards.

"There are a lot of people who get paid a lot for doing not much at all – like socialites on reality shows, or people who earn a million pounds a day working a couple of hours buying and selling shares," he told the *Daily Mirror*. "But what we earn we earn for doing an awful lot. We are constantly working."

Back in the States to promote their new album, they performed at *The X Factor USA* in the first week of November – the first time the lads had sung in front of Simon Cowell since the UK final of the show.

They also appeared on *The Ellen DeGeneres Show* in New York, where Harry took the opportunity to explain his latest tattoos: a pair of birds on his chest. "I got two little birdies," he said, "they're kind of like sailory, about, like, travelling. Birds fly. We fly a lot."

They went on to perform at an open-air gig at Manhattan's Rockefeller Center to 15,000 fans, filmed for the *Today* show, where Niall revealed the band were to follow in the footsteps of the Spice Girls and star in their own film. "We are going to do our first ever movie and it's going to be in 3D and it's coming to cinemas near you on August 13, 2013," he said, adding excitedly, "It'll be like we're in the room with you."

When he heard they were in LA, *Pirates Of the Caribbean* star Johnny Depp invited them over to his house as a treat for his 13-year-old daughter, Lily Rose, who was a big fan of the boys. Johnny also picked up a guitar to jam with them in his recording studio. But amazingly, Zayn didn't go with the others because he was too nervous about meeting the movie star.

"I am a massive, massive fan and I didn't want to embarrass myself so I let the boys go without me," he later told *The Sun*. "Hopefully, there will be a next time. The boys said he was totally cool. I kind of regret it for sure and the lads said I was a scaredy cat."

Harry returned to *The X Factor* studios in LA when Taylor Swift was rehearsing for her performance there. As the show's host, Mario Lopez, revealed: "Taylor Swift was the guest and during rehearsals, Harry came and slapped me on the back and said, 'Hey, Mario, how ya doing?' And I said, 'What are you doing here?' And he sort of pointed toward Taylor. They walked away hand in hand." Harry sat with Taylor's mother, Andrea, to watch her rehearsing and was later seen carrying Taylor back to her trailer.

On one subsequent day in LA, a charitable Harry spent nearly £3,000 of his money on pizzas and drove around handing them out to homeless people. Also, on a visit to the Shamrock Tattoo Shop on Sunset Boulevard that added to their body art, Zayn had more inking done on his 'half sleeve' design and Louis had a compass tattoo added to an array of images on his right arm.

One other amusing incident in LA occurred at a meeting to discuss their second album with music executives. The boys were sitting outside in a car, waiting to go in, when an attractive woman walked by. Acting more like building site workers than pop stars, they leant out of the window, calling, "Wah-hey!" and beeping the car horn to get her attention. Louis had them all laughing when, as she entered the building, he shouted, "What a bottom!"

But they had red faces when, after telling the woman she had "a sexy bum", they sat down for their meeting only to find her chairing it. She was one of the bosses of the record company!

"She was smiley about it and took it as a compliment," Liam recalled. "She said: 'I think we have already met outside.'" Simon Cowell later reprimanded the boys for their antics and Liam tweeted: "We have been properly told off."

*Take Me Home* shot to the top of the charts in 32 countries, including the US and UK, and the single 'Little Things', written by Ed Sheeran, also topped the UK charts. Zayn received a text message that read: "Congratulations, superstar." It was from his mum, Trisha. "Thanks, mom and pop," he texted back.

But there was a nasty exchange of words between Zayn and Max George of the Wanted towards the end of the month which was to escalate. Rival Brit boy band the Wanted had peaked at number two in the singles chart in America with 'Glad You Came', but had been eclipsed by the phenomenal success of One Direction.

In an interview with *Top Of The Pops* magazine, the Wanted were asked if they were worried about One Direction's success. Max replied: "Not at all because they are so different. They make me feel old! They're doing great and their music and videos are perfect for their market."

The Wanted's Siva Kaneswaran added: "Those boys have got their own thing going on. We've got a different music and I think it speaks for itself." So far, so good. But in another interview they branded One Direction's music as "for children", and said that its main aim was to "sell posters".

In an interview with *The Sun*, in September 2012, Liam had talked about how he didn't think the Wanted were rivals and why he felt disappointed by their attacks on One Direction: "The Wanted? I don't think there's any real competition between us. They sing dance music. They're real lads' lads, whereas we're just mischievous, which I think is different. For me, you just look at Twitter followers, which I think is a big player. The only thing that's bad for me about them is actually they were really nice to our faces, but when it came to talking to the media they were really trashy about us. We'd never done anything wrong. We were just running around doing our thing. We'd never purposely talk trash about anyone and we still haven't said anything about them now."

But that was to change when, in November, Zayn commented on a picture that Max was using as his display on Twitter, which showed him standing with R&B star Usher. Zayn called him a "geek". Max replied, tongue in cheek, "That's not very nice. I was just starting to like you and your RnB songs, too."

Zayn followed up with: "I'm not sure why your [sic] still talking to me mate conversation ended when I called you a geek. Your display just show's [sic] how much of a wannabe you are."

Max replied: "Tell me your problems without the 8 security in NYC. The only problem I have with you is the shit banter. Grow up son."

Zayn replied to Max: "I'd fucking love to. See you in New York big man. Ha. U clown."

When the Wanted's Tom Parker joined in, Zayn told him: "Let's not even start discussing vocal ability boys;) I would love to chat. Gotta run though to rehearsals."

Max replied: "Enjoy rehearsals. Stay off the bud... It clearly makes u cranky.'

To which Zayn replied: "Alright chlamydia boy."

Things were getting more and more childish and nasty. Tom wrote that Zayn had his "knickers in a twist".

Zayn told him: "Mate if I had a face like yours my hair would be the last thing I'd worry about:)"

Then Louis Tomlinson entered the fray to tell Tom: "Pipe down bad boy."

★ ★ ★

Back in the UK, One Direction performed at the prestigious Royal Variety Performance before the Queen, on November 19, 2012, singing 'Little Things'. Other singers on the show included Kylie Minogue, Rod

Stewart, Neil Diamond, Girls Aloud, Robbie Williams, Alicia Keys and Placido Domingo.

The boys were eagerly looking forward to playing at Madison Square Garden on December 3. Their trip back across the water would prove to be a romantic time for four of them, who were reunited with their loves.

Harry met up with Taylor Swift and they enjoyed a romantic stroll, hand in hand through Central Park, prior to the show. Liam had got back with Danielle Peazer, who flew out to New York to see him; they too held hands as they strolled along Fifth Avenue, stopping to look through the window of a jewellery shop.

Liam's family also flew out to see him, visiting such landmarks as the Empire State Building together. Perrie Edwards flew out to spend some time with Zayn, as did his family, while Louis and Eleanor were also seen shopping hand-in-hand. Niall's parents, Bobby and Maura, and brother Greg flew over for the gig, along with a number of Niall's closest friends from Mullingar.

One Direction performed in front of 20,000 fans at Madison Square Garden; it was a night they would never forget. One girl hurled her bra at Harry Styles, who spun it around on his finger and tossed it into the air. Fans also got an extra treat when special guest Ed Sheeran made an appearance.

During the gig, Zayn told the crowd: "I'm overwhelmed. I'm from a small town in Bradford. Things like this don't happen to people like me. I owe it all to you."

Niall Horan said: "It's always been a dream of mine to say, 'Hello, Madison Square Garden,'" and he told the ecstatic crowd, "This is the best night of our lives. You guys have travelled from all around the world and we cannot believe what has happened here tonight. Thank you so much."

Afterwards, Niall tweeted: "Wow, Madison Square Garden. Thank you so much. It was THE BEST NIGHT OF our lives. Thank you, thank you, thank you."

Harry tweeted: "It was the best thing I have ever done." And Liam wrote: "What a night! I had soooo much fun. Thank you to everyone who came to see us and every one of our fans who support us! I love you loads :)"

At the after-show party at the Hudson Hotel, a loved-up Harry and Taylor Swift duetted at a karaoke session featuring the Elton John and Kiki Dee song, 'Don't Go Breaking My Heart', and the Kenny Rogers and Dolly Parton classic, 'Islands In The Stream'. Taylor also sang with One Direction and Ed Sheeran on the Backstreet Boys' 1998 hit, 'I Want It That Way', while Ed and the One Direction boys covered Vanilla Ice's 'Ice Ice Baby'.

As a hotel employee reveals: "Everyone was going for it. They were on a high after one of the biggest nights of their lives and were intent on letting their hair down. They all looked pleased to have their loved ones – girlfriends, family and friends – with them and everyone was just having fun.

"Harry and Taylor sat cuddling each other for much of the time, gazing into each other's eyes. And Liam, Louis and Zayn were also enjoying the company of their girls. Niall, though, was loudly messing around with his pals.

"There was a lot of encouragement going on to take part in the karaoke. And everyone cheered when someone got up and after they had finished singing. It was a fun night."

Louis fell foul of US traffic cops once more, when they spotted him standing with his top half out of the sunroof of a moving car, filming himself on camera. They pulled the car over and gave him a dressing down. But Louis was filming scenes for the band's new 3D movie and, when the cops realised who he was, they posed for pictures with him and Niall, who was also in the car.

The Atlantic crossing continued as the boys returned to London to play at Capital FM's Jingle Bell Ball at London's O₂ arena, on December 8. Also on the bill were JLS and Will.i.am, who duetted with Cheryl Cole.

Harry had not travelled back with them but instead flew in with Taylor on a private jet she had arranged. Taylor was backstage to watch in a VIP area out of sight of the fans. The day after the show, he whisked her away for a brief but romantic break to the Lake District, where they laughingly fed the doves and swans in the picturesque town square of Bowness-on-Windermere, Cumbria.

The pair happily posed for lots of pictures for surprised and delighted locals and tourists. As jewellery shop manager Claire Dibbs described: "They were just walking past and one of my colleagues saw them. I ran outside and grabbed my phone for a picture. Harry was posing for another photo and Taylor was just hanging back. She thought I wanted to speak to just Harry! She introduced herself. She was really lovely. She said they were just here for the day."

Before leaving, Harry and Taylor bought some gifts from the Beatrix Potter shop for their families. Harry then celebrated Taylor's 23rd birthday by taking her to a traditional British pub: the George & Dragon in Great Budworth, Cheshire. In a sweet gesture, he had 23 cupcakes made for her – one for every year of her life. He also took her to his local Chinese restaurant in Holmes Chapel.

On one of their earlier trips to the US, the boys had recorded an interview with chat show host Barbara Walters, who had included them collectively on her prestigious list of 'The 10 Most Fascinating People'. The show was aired on December 12; in it, the boys made many female hearts flutter after she asked them if they felt ready to get married and have children. All five replied that they did, with Zayn adding, "I have always wanted kids."

But it was Louis who was teased by the others on a day to day basis for going all gooey whenever he encountered babies and young children. He told them that because he had four sisters, he was desperate to have a little boy of his own one day.

★ ★ ★

Harry and Taylor sloped off to the Canyons Resort in Park City, Utah, just before Christmas 2012, for a mini skiing break along with her brother Austin. After a few days of skiing, she flew off for a sunshine break to Australia with her family while Harry returned to Holmes Chapel

For Christmas, Harry's mother, Anne, gave him a box, saying, "This is all I can get for you." When he opened it, a label proclaimed it as "the present for someone with everything… A belly button brush." Harry fell about laughing.

On Boxing Day, Harry watched Manchester United play at Old Trafford with fellow United fan Olly Murs. They beat Newcastle 4-3.

Niall, as usual, divided his time over the Christmas between his two parents. As was his tradition, he went to the pub on Christmas Eve and chilled out, watching a lot of television, on Christmas Day. He also spent some time at Ed Sheeran's house and played Monopoly, which the boys had recently got into on tour. Harry also visited Ed and insisted that they watch the movie *One Day*.

When they began watching it, Ed complained that it was just a romance. So Harry fast-forwarded it to the end where Anne Hathaway's character, Emma, has a tragic accident whilst riding a bike. "That's what happens," said Harry, and then – despite his having ruined the ending – they watched it from the start!

Liam arrived home in Wolverhampton late on Christmas Eve. Instead of a traditional meal of turkey, his family visited their favourite Indian restaurant, Penn Tandoori in Wolverhampton, on Christmas Day, where they enjoyed a shish kebab starter followed by a chicken tikka bhuna main course with rice and naan.

The restaurant manager, Jay Uddin, revealed: "We get quite a lot of bookings on Christmas Day. They had pre-booked to come at 2 p.m. [Liam] is a down to earth, normal guy. We just treat him like a regular customer but he seems like a friendly and nice lad.

"He is always polite and says thank you. He might be a millionaire but I think his dad might have paid for [the meal]." They also went out to the popular Tumbledown Farm carvery in Cannock over the festive break. Amongst Liam's family presents was the *Toy Story* movie box set, Batman merchandise, a model aeroplane, clothes and chocolates.

Meanwhile, Harry had been missing Taylor and he flew out to be with her on New Year's Eve. However, he very nearly didn't make it when, in his haste, he arrived at Heathrow only to realise he had left his passport behind. He had been driven to the airport by Anne on December 28 for an 11.15 a.m. flight to Boston, but had to send for a motorbike courier to bring it to him. It meant another eight-hour wait before boarding an evening flight.

Taylor was performing in New York's Times Square, alongside Justin Bieber and a host of other stars for the annual TV special *Dick Clark's New Year's Rockin' Eve*. Earlier in the evening, Harry and Taylor had watched Jay-Z and Coldplay's New Year's Eve concert in Brooklyn and kissed publicly amongst the crowd.

A few days later, the pair flew off for a romantic stay in the Caribbean on the island of Virgin Gorda, enjoying cocktails and dinner at the CocoMaya restaurant on the beach. With its white sandy beaches, coral reefs and clear, warm waters, it is a paradise island – perfect for lovers. But the idyll proved less than ideal when they fell out after a blazing row.

Sources say that Taylor was annoyed at the attention Harry was receiving, and irritated when he spent too much time chatting and drinking with other holidaymakers. She reportedly lost her temper and they had heated words.

Taylor cut short the holiday and flew home, but Harry stayed on and visited Richard Branson's nearby Necker Island for a party. When he flew back to Heathrow, however, he looked glum. He had taken it badly and neither party was inclined to ring the other to apologise.

There was immediate speculation in the media, after news of their split began circulating, that Harry might be vilified in a future Taylor Swift song. After all, she had a track record of attacking past loves in her lyrics. After Joe of the Jonas Brothers reportedly broke up with her over the phone, she wrote a song called 'Forever & Always' on her 2008 album *Fearless*. In a Myspace video of the song, she portrayed him with a *Camp Rock* doll – based on the character he plays in the 2008 Disney movie of the same name. In the video, she holds up the doll and says: "See, this one even comes with a phone, so he can break up with other dolls."

Her hit 'We Are Never Ever Getting Back Together' is rumoured to be about her split with actor Jake Gyllenhaal, and 'Dear John', on her 2010 album *Speak Now*, is based on her broken relationship with musician John Mayer. "I always write songs about my life," she once said. "And if you're horrible to me I'm going to write a song about you and you are not going to like it. That's how I operate."

★   ★   ★

There was some more cheering news when One Direction were nominated for a Brit Award for Best British Group in 2013.

In mid-January, they travelled to Accra, Ghana, as part of the annual UK charity telethon *Comic Relief*. Here they met poverty-stricken people who receive donations and support from Comic Relief projects in the region. It was to be an extremely moving experience for the boys, leaving them all in tears.

The most traumatic time was when they visited a hospital where babies were dying because they had no vaccines. Sick from malnutrition, pneumonia and other illnesses, the babies were almost lifeless in their mothers' arms. As Niall commented: "It's crazy what's going on in here." "That was the hardest thing I've ever had to do," Louis said of his conversations with nurses and mothers.

Harry tenderly held a newborn baby, and was there when a young boy was rushed in with malaria. He wasn't moving and was too weak to cry. Harry and Liam were heartbroken as they watched the little boy's mother holding her son, who was unable to hold his own head up.

Harry couldn't restrain the tears from streaming down his face. "It's so sad," said Liam as he and Harry walked out, unable to cope with their emotions. As Harry later said: "We all had moments. If you get involved in it and you don't cry you're superhuman. It's crazy how quick you get connections with children and people who live there. You feel upset leaving them and saying goodbye to them."

There were lighter moments for the group during the visit, as some boys playing football greeted them with calls of "Westlife!" All of the boys described the trip as the most amazing experience they ever had. Earlier in the year they had recorded a cover of Blondie's 'One Way Or Another' to raise money for the charity, which would be released at the end of January.

A few days later they made their first promotional visit to Japan. It seemed that everyone was aware of who they were, as a huge crowd turned up to greet them at Narita Airport in Tokyo. Getting into the spirit of things, the boys dressed in red kimonos to the delight of their fans.

It was a brief visit, but while they were there they enjoyed singing karaoke at a bar and eating sushi. They belted out some Jay-Z and 50 Cent numbers, plus the Backstreet Boys' 'I Want It That Way', Justin Bieber's 'As Long As You Love Me' and Aerosmith's 'I Don't Want To Miss A Thing'. Harry enthusiastically threw himself into 'Islands In The Stream' – which he had previously sung with Taylor Swift. With a big smile on his face, he looked like he had got over their recent split.

At a press conference the following day, the boys announced an extra two Japanese dates on their world tour later in the year. But Zayn mysteriously walked out halfway through the conference, leaving the others wondering what was wrong with him. Later they discovered that he had been sick. The late-night karaoke and beer carousing had caught up with him.

During some downtime, Zayn bought a robot that he spent hours assembling in his hotel room, much to the amusement of the others. Later that January, however, he was to be embroiled in a scandal that seriously threatened his relationship with Perrie Edwards. An Australian waitress named Courtney Webb told *The Sun* that, on a night out at a London nightclub called Dstrkt, a mutual friend named Leon Anderson invited her back to Zayn's six-bedroom house in north London for a party. Courtney, 21, hit it off with Zayn; according to her, she was about to leave at 5 a.m. when he told her she was "hot" and "beautiful", and asked her to stay.

She remained behind with him after all the other guests had gone, and later went to bed with him. Unfortunately for Zayn she had also taken some rather incriminating pictures of him asleep in his bed, which backed up her story. According to her, he had assured her that he was single, but she later spotted clothes and jewellery belonging to Perrie Edwards, and realised they were in a relationship.

Perrie was in Wales, busy rehearsing for Little Mix's UK and Ireland tour. When the story appeared in the press, Zayn was only too happy to fly out to Cannes with his bandmates to escape the fallout.

One Direction were performing the new single, 'Kiss You', at the NRJ (Nouvelle Radio des Jeunes) Music Awards. Harry was also feeling awkward because Taylor Swift was performing. The two managed to avoid each other, but singing her hit song, 'We Are Never Ever Getting Back Together', onstage in front of her ex-boyfriend seemed to be a pretty direct message.

One Direction took home the award for Best International Group, but Zayn was dreading facing the music with Perrie. He headed for Nottingham where Little Mix were performing, and the couple had a heart-to-heart in her room. He was later seen puffing nervously on a cigarette, getting into a cab with an ashen-faced Perrie. She studiously ignored looking at him, busying herself with a mirror to apply her make-up.

Harry celebrated his 19th party in London with a group of pals and was embarrassed when a strip-a-gram dressed as a sexy police officer – organised by his close friend, Radio 1 DJ Nick Grimshaw – stripped to her undies to perform a lap dance on him. She pushed his head into her ample chest as the other guests laughed at his discomfort.

One Direction's manager had rushed to cover up the CCTV cameras as soon as the stripper arrived, but some pictures were leaked to the newspapers anyway. Harry couldn't stop laughing when she later told him she couldn't find her police truncheon, so she'd brought along some nunchukas – oriental fighting sticks – instead. The laughter increased when one of the other men recognised her and told Harry, "I went to college with her!"

Meanwhile, Zayn had been battling to get back in Perrie's good books and was pulling out all the stops. When he went to watch her perform with Little Mix in Liverpool, he called out, "Love you Perrie!" from the audience. He also bought her a huge teddy bear emblazoned with the words "I love you" at a service station.

Days later, he turned up to rehearse for the approaching world tour wearing a jumper with a large letter 'P' on the front – a very public display of love. The other boys in the band were amused by it but thought better of teasing him, knowing that he was going through a difficult time.

At the Brit Awards in February, they performed their new single, 'One Way Or Another (Teenage Kicks)', for the first time. Such had been their undeniable worldwide achievement that they were awarded the Global Success Award.

But they proved not to be such a big hit with waspish Boy George, who took umbrage with Liam for an alleged snub. He tweeted: "Top marks to Harry Styles for stopping for a picture with my niece and bollocks to Liam and the disrespectful wanker of a minder."

Liam responded by tweeting that Boy George had not wanted to speak to *him* when he realised he wasn't Niall Horan: "Now now boy lets not tell porkies. Firstly thanks for getting my name wrong three times, then asking me where is Liam? ... awkward. Then when you finally got it right saying you wanted Niall instead.

"If you would have asked me for a picture I would have stopped bro. I just did what you said and pointed Niall out for you so u just keep wearing ur strange hats and enjoy yourself my little Georgie pie ... It's still not cool you just look weird."

It took Boy George 11 days to notice Liam's comment. Clearly enraged, he returned to Twitter to savage him for mocking his headwear: "I had no idea that twit Liam had made some dig about my hat!" he wrote. "Lucky I'm a Buddhist or I'd crack the twat!"

The One Direction boys also reacted to the views of the Dylan-esque British singer and songwriter Jake Bugg on Twitter. In an interview with GQ the previous year, Bugg said: "I don't care about the word 'pop'... sadly what's popular today is mostly manufactured and commercial and all about fame and looks and boy bands. It's not on. One Direction? The young girls will grow up and forget about 'em."

He was to lay into them again in an interview after the Brits, calling for an end to comparisons with the Beatles. "People call One Direction the new Beatles because they broke America, but that don't mean a thing. I mean, they must know that they're terrible," Jake told *Shortlist* magazine. "They must know ... calling them the new rock stars is a ridiculous statement. And people should stop making it."

Niall took to Twitter to write: "Really buggs me that artists we're fans of, flip on us in the press !" And Louis sarcastically commented: "Hi @JakeBugg do you think slagging off boy bands makes you more indie?"

Never mind. The gleam from the Global Success award was enough to give them comfort. But it was only the start of their dominance of the world stage...

# 12

# World Domination

One Direction's *Take Me Home* world tour started at London's O$_2$ Arena on February 23, 2013. It would see them playing in country after country on 117 dates, all the way through to November 2013 when it came to an end in Japan. Such had been the demand for tickets that all venues were sell-outs.

They arrived onstage at the O$_2$ in spectacular style – suspended on wires. Then, before a backdrop of the London skyline including Big Ben and the towering Shard, their two-hour show included at least eight costume changes.

The boys immediately got the crowd singing along with their hit single 'Up All Night'. Later, they raised some laughs with video footage which included Louis in a fat suit, asking people on the street for a hug, and all of them dressed as pensioners. Zayn encouraged the audience to wave glow sticks as the band sat on a raised platform to sing 'Little Things', accompanied by Niall on the guitar.

Mindful of the debt they owed to Twitter, they once again included a Q&A. The questions may have been trivial, but no one cared. Such communication with their fans had been a vital part of their success from the start and it was a fun element. The audience learned – if they didn't already know – that Harry's favourite

Disney movie was *Dumbo* and his favourite Italian food was pasta carbonara.

Of course, even such seemingly innocuous revelations carried the risk of being bombarded with cuddly elephants and pasta in the future. Louis had already learned that a jokey line about liking carrots could have severe repercussions!

The tour included spoof video footage in the interlude entitled 'The Morning After': it showed Niall waking up on the sofa with a moustache and beard drawn on his face; 'Daddy Liam' in an apron depicting a bare muscular torso, wiping down the kitchen surfaces wearing rubber washing-up gloves; Zayn waking up outside and finding himself in a yellow chicken outfit; Louis walking into the bathroom – past a goat – and seeing Harry soaking in the bath, wearing a bath hat.

The impressive O$_2$ Arena carried memories for Liam. When he introduced their hit 'More Than This', he looked around the venue and commented: "This place is absolutely huge. I came here to watch Jay Z and Kayne West. I came here to watch Robbie Williams. And now we are here."

Amongst the audience was Harry's parents and his 77-year-old grandfather, Brian. Although Brian's daughter, Anne, was worried that he might find it a bit noisy, he ended up loving it.

"Harry is a wonderful performer," Brian told the *Sunday Mirror*. "I was so impressed seeing him live for the first time. It was absolutely brilliant. The boys were fantastic and I couldn't have been more proud. My daughter Anne was concerned before the concert that the noise would be too loud for me but I would really like to go again."

And he stressed that, despite Harry's fame, "He's still the same. He always has a smile on his face and is very loving and caring. We're all lucky to have him. To me he's just lovable Harry. I don't think of him as this well-known pop star like everyone else."

At the O$_2$ gig, Louis had make a jokey comment to the fans about the two acts who had been critical of them when he remarked that "Jake Bugg was supporting the Wanted". This upset Tom Parker of the Wanted, who hit out at Louis on Twitter: "You even talk about us at your own gigs. Are you that upset you didn't get in this band?"

Louis responded: "Pal, we both know I wouldn't waste my time auditioning for your band. You humour me [sic] with your bad boy persona."

Other members of both bands then joined in. It escalated so much that even some of their girlfriends had a say! Tom posted a link of Louis' *X Factor* audition, implying he couldn't sing: "You were too busy 'wowing the judges' with THIS."

And Louis posted some pictures of Tom, underneath which he had written sarcastic captions such as "bad boys for life" and "my idol". Later he added a link to an old interview where Tom revealed he had failed to get through an *X Factor* audition. He then called Tom the "biggest t*** on Twitter", adding, "Why don't we make your next single our movie soundtrack?"

Tom shot back: "Hmm, I'd love to make the soundtrack to *Mean Girls 3*."

Referring to Tom's bandmate Max George's rumoured romance with *Mean Girls* actress Lindsay Lohan, Louis replied: "Not a bad idea actually. Maybe @MaxTheWanted could ask Lindsay?"

At the mention of his name, Max tweeted: "Louis Tomlinson. Sorry did you want me?"

Then it was the turn of the usually diplomatic and mild-mannered Liam to join ranks with Louis: "Hey Tom, let's talk about your singing. Your amazing tone pierces my ears with every note :/ p.s. tweet out when you have someone to speak to. Our drummer has more followers than you."

Louis added another dig at Tom: "I also heard he wets the bed."

When Tom's girlfriend, Kelsey Hardwick, re-tweeted a message from a fan criticising Louis, Eleanor Calder was stung into action. She simply tweeted: "KelseyBelle90 #NipSlip", referring to a photograph of her that had been in the newspapers showing an unfortunate slip with one of her boobs, popping out of her top, on a night out with Tom.

Kelsey sarcastically replied to her: "Awwww bless ya!!! Did ya wanna see more!!xxx"

The Wanted's Jay McGuiness then wrote a lengthy, measured and articulate post – of the like seldom seen on Twitter – hoping to stop the war of words: "Dear @Louis_Tomlinson, please stop mentioning us in your gigs, we certainly no longer mention you and it's time to let dead dogs lie. Your passive-aggressive style of speaking makes me cringe, and I wish you'd either have the bollocks of some of your co-workers to speak truthfully, or the class of the majority of them to be silent.

"I'm not sure what's happened since we saw you at *The X Factor*, but you've done a sterling job of becoming one of the most overrated, arrogant and not to mention insincere people around.

"Your shocking lack of talent will only be forgiven by lots of humility and no-strings-attached friendship among your band.

"Louis, don't measure your worth in followers or money, because they're fickle, and when they go you might just feel worthless."

Louis made sure he had the last word in replying to Tom: "You clearly spend too much time on Twitter. Funny that face to face you act like a little girl." He added: "You must have been a splendid student. Never forget you boys started this."

But if anyone thought that was an end to it, they were very much mistaken. The following month, mischievous Max questioned Louis' sexuality in an interview with US TV show *Watch What Happens Live*. After mentioning One Direction, the host, Andy Cohen, jokingly asked Max, "Who do you think will be the first to come out?" Max instantly replied, "Louis."

The Wanted had appeared to be attempting to mend fences earlier, during an interview in the US with Katie Couric on her show. Max had said: "There has been a bit of Twitter arguing and all that sort of stuff… because we're so mature. There's a little bit of bad feeling with a couple of the boys from another band. That's about as far as I'm going to go with it. We haven't seen them to actually talk face to face, but we'd like to at some point because I'm sure underneath all the front and the bitchiness they're actually pretty nice people. [Though] I've yet to see it."

Louis later sounded like he was in conciliatory mode about the bust-up – before sticking the knife in again: "I think it is always blown up out of proportion, the way that just because we're two boy bands there's massive rivalry," he said in an interview. "But we are hoping that they'll still get on with us. Because, you know, there is potentially a spot on our arena tour for them to support us."

Hostilities were to flare once more later in the year, when Max George of the Wanted suggested that they should have a boxing match: "them against us." He went on: "It would be brilliant for TV and I have no problem with it at all. They've got 12 million followers on Twitter and I get that they have an army of kids. But instead of doing that if they have got an issue, why don't we actually do something financially – like make some money for a charity, and blow off some steam in a boxing ring?"

His bandmate Jay McGuiness doubted that the two groups will ever be friends: "We haven't spoken. I think no matter how much you try to avoid it, people are always gearing up for, you know, what do you think of them, what do they think of you?

"It's going to be really hard to ever have a real friendship and we don't see them enough for that. We're not going to lose any sleep over it."

★   ★   ★

Back on the tour, in Glasgow there was a missile thrown at the stage – not a carrot, a bowl of pasta or a cuddly toy, but a shoe. Unfortunately, it hit Harry just where he least needed it – in the crotch. He doubled up in pain but gamely managed to continue.

Liam saw the funny side of it, shouting, "Man down, man down!" Later, 14-year-old Jade Anderson from Kilbride stepped forward to confess it was her who put her foot in it. But she insisted that she never meant to hurt Harry. "I never thought I'd hit him. I just wanted the boys to touch my shoes," she told the *Scottish Sun*. "I wish I could hug him and say sorry."

Jade had thrown both of her shoes on the stage. "The boys were so close and I wanted them to touch something of mine so I climbed up on my seat and threw one shoe. But the second one caught Harry. Then security dragged me away. I didn't mean any harm and just got too excited but it was scary when I was marched out the hall."

She was warned that it was technically an assault, but Harry came to her rescue by asking security staff to let her back in. Jade rejoined the audience 10 minutes later. One of her shoes was returned when Niall handed it to security, but she had to search for the other one at the end of the gig, and eventually found it. Jade's mother, Angela, was at home when a friend posted on Facebook to tell her what had happened. Angela said: "She is a huge fan and really regrets it."

As the tour schedule was so intense, One Direction travelled in style in order to get to so many locations on time. Hiring their own private jet, they flew onto Cardiff. It was a short pop and even Louis couldn't blame jet lag for forgetting his words halfway through the performance. When it came to his solo part in the cover of 'Teenage Dirtbag', he lost the plot and the others had to hurriedly cover for him After the song, an embarrassed Louis mumbled, "I'm sorry, Cardiff." Later, he admitted, "I just forgot the lyrics."

But his time in Dublin proved to be particularly memorable and far more pleasant. Louis' mother, Jay, had come over to watch him perform; while they were both in Dublin, her boyfriend, Dan Deakin, proposed to her. Louis was delighted when she told him the news. He had always been concerned about her since her divorce, and his breakthrough with One Direction that had kept him away from home. Wherever he was in the world, he would text his mother up to seven times a day. He was living the dream but, as the eldest of her children, felt a nagging guilt that he had left her behind to cope with the family on her own.

There was one more (less pleasant) reason for Louis to remember the Irish leg of the tour: he injured his knee in Belfast and had to hobble around the stage.

During a break in their schedule, the band joined in with the live fundraising *Comic Relief* night on British TV. Footage of their trip to Africa was shown, followed by a rousing live performance in the studio of 'One Way Or Another (Teenage Kicks)'. Louis got into the swing of the event – in which the symbol is a clown's red nose – by dyeing his hair red after Doncaster Rovers FC petitioned him to do so on Twitter.

Back on the road, tragedy struck when they moved on to Liverpool, where a stage hand suffered a head injury and collapsed while preparing for the show at the Echo Arena. He was rushed to hospital where he later died.

Performing once more at London's O$_2$ Arena, Liam crept up behind Harry as he was singing onstage and yanked his trousers down, revealing his black underwear to the delight of the sell-out crowd, who screamed their approval. Harry carried on singing, yanking them back up with one hand, but looked clearly uncomfortable – which was a little ironic, given his exhibitionist tendencies!

When the tour moved on to Sheffield, Louis took the opportunity to spend a couple of days back home with his family in Doncaster, attempting to get back to a normal life – up to a point, anyway. A camera crew followed him to record footage for inclusion in their forthcoming film, to be called *This Is Us*. Louis caused a stir when he picked up his younger sister, Phoebe, from Willow Primary School. The cameras also followed him to Hall Cross and Hayfield schools, and when he went to visit his 90-year-old great-grandmother, Olive.

A large contingent of Louis' family and friends – around 60 in all, including Olive – went to watch him perform in Sheffield. Louis viewed it as his hometown show, as did Zayn – whose family were also there because it was not far from their hometown of Bradford.

Harry brought along a two-wheeled electric-powered Segway vehicle to the Motorpoint Area in Sheffield, where he had fun riding on it backstage. The other boys in the band also had a go and had a lot of fun spinning around on it. But then high-spirited Harry decided to have more fun by going streaking.

"We were all having fun doing spins when he suddenly stripped off," Louis told *The Sun*. "He turned a few heads."

Niall added: "He's a braver boy than me. It can get a bit chilly when you pick up speed. It can be quite cold backstage too."

A radio competition caused havoc in the Payne household, after it hid two tickets to the sell-out One Direction concert in Birmingham. The idea was that a series of cryptic clues would lead listeners to the tickets, but when the clues were misinterpreted by fans around 100 excited fans swarmed all over the garden of Liam's family home in Wolverhampton. They searched in bushes, pot plants and under wheelie bins. The tickets were later found taped to the back of a nearby road sign.

"I've had people loitering around the house for days on end now. I'm glad someone won it," said Liam's father, Geoff. "There have been people hiding round corners looking for them."

Despite almost continuous snowfall throughout the day, there wasn't an empty seat at the NEC arena in Birmingham. Harry drove the fans wild when, midway through 'Rock Me', he started swirling the microphone around before throwing it to the floor like a latter-day Mick Jagger. Liam just waved and spoke to his family from the stage, asking how they were doing.

A few days later, One Direction won in two categories at that year's Nickelodeon Kids Choice Awards in Los Angeles – Favourite Music Group and Favourite Song for 'What Makes You Beautiful' – but were unable to attend because of the tour. Perrie Edwards was there with Little Mix though, and she described One Direction to TV reporters as "amazing".

Louis was upset shortly afterwards by the *Sunday Mirror*, when it carried an interview with his estranged father, Troy Austin. Troy, 44, told how Louis' half-sister, Georgia, 14, was a huge One Direction fan and how he'd bought tickets for her and himself to watch their gig at Nottingham. Troy, who had lost touch with both his son and with ex-wife Jay, said he last saw Louis over two years ago, when he'd got in touch to tell him he was appearing on *The X Factor*.

"Seeing Louis on that stage was amazing," he told the newspaper. "He's in the biggest band in the world and I'm the proudest dad in the world. I just hope he knows it."

Troy said that Louis had only seen Georgia three times, and how they'd hoped to go backstage afterwards for a reunion but were told the band had to "rush off", which left her disappointed. "I haven't been there for most of his life, so I understand I'm not one of his main priorities. He knows we were in the crowd and now I want to tell him what it meant to me to see him up there. I cried buckets."

Troy added: "Seeing what he's done with his life makes me so happy. I know people will think I'm only interested in being part of his life again because he's rich and famous. But it's not about that.

"I'm his dad. We're flesh and blood and nothing can change that. I'm so proud of him I could burst. Of course, I would love to see him again and have a proper relationship with him. What dad wouldn't? But it's up to him."

Louis reacted furiously to the article and hit out on Twitter: "I'd like to start off the day by saying a big fuck you to 'the mirror' :) on a happier note huge love to all our fans, you keep us going!!"

During a few days off from touring, Liam took the opportunity to watch a football match between Brazil and Russia at Chelsea's Stamford Bridge stadium, with his pal Andy Samuels. Sitting in a cab on the way to the ground, One Direction's 'One Way Or Another (Teenage Kicks)' came on the radio and the driver promptly turned it off! Andy fell about laughing.

Meanwhile, Liam's girlfriend, Danielle, delighted his fans when she posted a picture on Twitter of the husky puppy dog they had recently bought, wearing a Batman outfit! Superhero fan Liam had named the dog Loki, after the villainous character played by Tom Hiddleston in *Avengers Assemble*. He was delighted when Tom mentioned it in his speech at the MTV Movie Awards in April, where he was voted Best Villain: "I just want to thank Liam Payne from One Direction who I believe has named his dog Loki," he said. "Liam's dog Loki is unquestionably better looking, certainly better bred and probably better known. He has probably got more Twitter followers than I have!"

At the *Billboard* Music Awards in Las Vegas, One Direction were voted Top New Artist, Top Group and Top Pop Artist in their absence.

Meanwhile, Niall was best man for his brother Greg when he married beautician Denise Kelly at a local church in Mullingar. Niall's attendance attracted a sizeable crowd of onlookers. While in town, he delighted regulars at the pub when he took along his guitar and sang 'Little Things'.

Back with the band in Newcastle, Niall and the others got the giggles when Liam dropped his microphone off the stage while singing

'Summer Love'. They were all still giggling well into the next song, 'Little Things.'

At the beginning of the year, One Direction had found time to sit for the famous Madame Tussauds waxwork museum in London. Now, in April 2013, the models appeared remarkably lifelike when they were unveiled, seated at two benches. Harry thought they were "amazing" and deemed it "such an honour". Niall was a little spooked by the accuracy. "This is weird," he said. "He's wearing my actual shoes."

Five different sculptors worked on their individual heads, which took about five weeks to complete, while other sculptors worked on the bodies. Georgina Power, who sculpted Louis, explained the process:

"With each wax figure, and in the case of Louis, we start with a brief which our stylist provided for us. It sets the wheels in motion for a sitting. We've got them for 90 minutes and within that time we collect 200 measurements and 200 photos and we bring that all back to the studio where I was to start the process of sculpting Louis' head.

"Each head starts off with a metal armature. Then we put the clay on and we work to a profile that we would have taken at the fitting, which is a shot of Louis from five metres away. And then, using the measurements and the photos, we hope to capture the expression as best we can.

"One unique thing about sculpting the One Direction boys is that we've got five of them and their eye angle all had to be in the same direction. The bench has two levels and we were meeting each of the guys on separate days. And getting all of that to link up at the end, to get the result that we want, is pretty tricky. But the guys were great and we had a really good team working on it. And I think we nailed it."

Senior sculptor David Burks, who worked on Niall, had some difficulty in calming his subject's enthusiasm. "During the sitting Niall was so impressed that he couldn't sit still, which was a bit tricky for me because I needed him to do the same pose as in the portrait," he recalled. "But he started sculpting himself, so I had to stop him so I could finish him off. He was just really interested in the process."

166

Alex Carlisle was keen to capture the 'niceness' of Liam. "After the first sitting it was clear to me that he was a really nice, kind guy and I wanted to get some of that expression into his pose," he explained.

Principal sculptor Steve Mansfield also thought that Zayn was "a nice bloke" and "really helpful in the sitting. He did the pose brilliantly."

But prankster Harry had sculptor Jim Kempton worried when, as he was putting the finishing touches to his clay head, he commented: "Do you know what, Jim? I really don't think this is working. We're going to have to start again." As panic began to set in, Harry started laughing, much to Jim's relief.

★　★　★

As fans of *Scooby Doo*, for the American arm of their tour One Direction thought it would be great fun to travel around in the famous crime-solving team's Mystery Machine. So work began on customising an old Volkswagen campervan to resemble the iconic turquoise-and-yellow van.

Later that month, One Direction were named as Britain's richest boy band, with a combined wealth of £25 million, in the *Sunday Times* Rich List for 2013.

Pleased by Louis' frequent mentions of Yorkshire Tea, the parent company sponsored him to take girlfriend Eleanor on a romantic train journey aboard the luxurious Orient Express. They also invited his mother, Jay, and her fiancé, Dan Deakin.

In between tour dates, One Direction managed to start working on their third album, which was due to come out in time for Christmas stockings. The boys had a 10-day break after their final UK gig in Manchester on April 19, before the tour moved on to mainland Europe.

In the interim Harry flew out to Los Angeles, where he was seen having dinner at Dan Tana's restaurant in West Hollywood with 33-year-old Kimberly Stewart. But it was a family 'triple date', as Kimberly's rock star father, Rod Stewart, was also there with his wife, Penny Lancaster, along with Rod's son Sean and his girlfriend, Adrienne Maloof.

The gathering seemed to underline the notion that age doesn't matter when it comes to relationships. Kimberly – mother to 20-month-old daughter Delilah with Benecio del Toro – was 14 years older than 19-year-old Harry. But then Rod was 26 years older than Penny and Adrienne 20 years older than Sean.

There was much speculation about whether Harry and Kimberly's relationship was just a friendship, or whether it was something more. But Rod later spilled the beans in an interview on Alan Carr's *Chatty Man* show.

When asked about their relationship, Rod let slip: "[Harry's] car was here [at Rod's LA mansion] in the morning. Let's put it that way. But he may just have come round to pick something up." Then, realising he had said too much, Rod exclaimed, "Bollocks. I let the cat out of the bag."

As the tour moved on to mainland Europe, the boys had some difficulty during the Q&A session in Paris, when they were asked to greet the crowd in French with the line, "Hello we're One Direction and we're happy to see you." Prior to the concert, they visited the Eiffel Tower and also enjoyed a game of football. It aggravated Niall's old football injury, however, which left him limping when they moved on to Antwerp and Amsterdam.

The boys had become particularly fond of a steak restaurant in Paris called Le Relais de l'Entrecote, where they enjoyed large portions of steak and chips. On the French Radio station NRJ, they were asked about how life had changed for them. Zayn replied: "Yeah, life's crazy. About two years ago we were all students at school so to be doing this is crazy."

The boys were still truly shocked at the reception they received everywhere, and how much had happened in such a short space of time. "It's weird to take in because you feel you are doing so much but you haven't got enough time to do it all," said Zayn on a TV station in Denmark.

A huge crowd swarmed round them as they went shopping in Amsterdam. The boys had used Twitter to ask fans to wear orange – the colour of the Dutch royal family – at their concert, and loud screams rang out when One Direction walked on wearing orange suits.

But once more, the amount of time Liam was spending apart from girlfriend Danielle Peazer took its toll, and they decided to split up again. While she went off to Dubai with friends for a holiday, Liam's pal Andy Samuels flew over to spend time with him and they enjoyed a thrilling speedboat trip on the next leg of the tour in Norway.

Harry was startled when he emerged from his hotel and a girl ran past security guards to hug him. She laughed as she was pulled away, and a cheer rang out from a crowd of girls.

While in Oslo, Harry let his hair down by partying with a bus full of students until the early hours of the morning. They were taking part in a traditional Norwegian pre-graduation party known as 'Russ' (*Russefeiring* – celebration).

When one of the students saw Harry having dinner at his hotel, she asked if she could take a picture of him; she also told him about the party on the bus and asked if he wanted to join them.

Fellow student Michelle Fjeld-Hansen, 19, told *E! News*: "Harry got on the bus around midnight and we just kind of partied. Everyone jumps around and spills beer and everyone kind of gets wet and your hair gets crazy. We poured beer on him to welcome him. He really had a good time." She said that his bodyguards drove behind them the entire time he was on the bus, until he left about 3 a.m.

In Zurich, Zayn and Liam told a TV interviewer that they had grown up a lot since the beginning of One Direction. "My friends actually say that to me," said Zayn. "They say I'm a lot more mature since I've been in the band and stuff. I think it's just you're exposed to a lot more situations that you might not have been exposed to before."

Liam felt he had also gained in confidence. "One of the things I have learned about being in this position is that when I used to go to parties and someone came up to talk to you and you didn't really know them, I wouldn't be able to hold a conversation," he remarked. "I'm not really that shy any more. Me and Zayn were actually really quiet when we came into the band but now you can't shut us up."

In the romantic city of Verona, Italy, where One Direction played at their oldest venue to date – the 2,000-year-old Verona Arena – Zayn was joined by Perrie Edwards.

When they moved on to Germany, the boys visited the remains of the Berlin Wall – apart from Louis, who was feeling a little unwell. At the concert, he was noticeably coughing and spluttering on some songs and the others had to cover for him.

Living in each other's pockets for almost three years might be enough to strain anyone's friendship, yet the boys insisted they hardly ever argued. When they did, it was always about some trivial thing which would blow over very quickly – usually when one or other started laughing at the silliness of the situation.

"We all get on really well and just have a laugh," Liam told *Top Of The Pops* magazine. "It's like a group of kids at school having private jokes that the teachers aren't in on.

"I'm not going to lie and say that we don't have arguments because everyone has arguments, especially when you're all thrown together into a situation, but it's surprising how well we do get on."

Harry had previously remarked on how their few arguments were inconsequential: "To be honest, we don't argue very much at all. If we do, it's about silly things like where we're going for dinner."

Niall agreed, but added, "But if anyone's likely to bicker in the group, it would be Louis!"

Concerned that the boys would be too reliant on an unhealthy fast foot diet, their management team hired personal chef Sarah Nicholas and her team to cook for them on their travels. Ms Nicholas told the *Daily Star* that they liked to eat at 5.30 p.m. every day. "We always make sure we've got vegetables and there is always a juicer out," she said. "They have a choice of healthy food. They are very aware of what to eat and a trainer helps them out.

"Liam likes his bacon, steak and vegetables, while Louis eats anything – but a bowl of Special K is his favourite. Zayn is very easy to please. He just likes a pasta with Bolognese or spicy chicken. He is not a foodie and eats whatever's going. Niall likes more simple food, like sausage and mash, pies, creamy chicken pasta or chicken Kiev."

As for drinks, they preferred fruit juices to fizzy drinks. "Before they go on stage, they tend to have orange or apple juice, Capri-Suns or Rubicon.

"Yorkshire tea bags are a must. Louis is the main tea-drinker – he's from Doncaster so he loves Yorkshire tea the most."

In the midst of their mega-tour, the boys flew back to the UK to announce a world stadium tour in 2014, which would see them playing to huge crowds in new territories, particularly in Latin America. At the Wembley Stadium press conference, the first 13 dates of the Where We Are Tour were disclosed, which would see them performing in Colombia, Peru, Paraguay, Chile, Argentina, Uruguay and Brazil, followed by UK gigs in Dublin, Sunderland, Manchester, Edinburgh and Wembley itself. More dates would be announced later, including a US leg.

"We're massively excited because there's a lot of places around the world that we haven't been to and we can't wait to get over there," said Liam. "It's important for the fans to know it's not just the same 'Take Me Home Tour' going around in stadiums."

Niall was, as ever, even more excited. "We are ecstatic," he said. "We have only been a band for three years and we're already doing stadiums – including Wembley. And the thought of stepping out to an audience of 65,000 a night is incredible."

Harry added: "It's important the fans and everyone who comes to see the show know it's going to be much bigger and [with] new songs. A completely different tour."

During the press conference, they also talked about their forthcoming album. "It's taken a slightly rockier tone," said Louis.

"We made it a lot more edgier," Liam added.

One Direction later announced that 50p from all ticket sales in UK and Ireland from the tour would be donated to the Stand Up To Cancer charity. This was estimated to be worth around £200,000.

"Cancer affects nearly everyone at some point in their lives so we all need to do what we can to bring forward the day when all cancers are cured," said Liam.

Shortly afterwards, Harry's Radio One DJ pal, Nick Grimshaw, told *The Independent* that he didn't think One Direction would be an appropriate act for the prestigious Glastonbury Festival. They had not been invited to take part at the event in June anyway, but there had been speculation. "I don't think One Direction's music sounds like the stuff that is historically supported by Glastonbury," added Grimshaw.

The boys were also snubbed by a snooty doorman who refused them entry to a London nightspot, 5 Hertford Street, for not being smartly enough dressed. Despite people telling the doorman that they knew who the famous five were, he was not impressed when they enlightened him, commenting, "They're going in one direction, and that's away from here." The exclusive members' club, launched in 2012, has a membership which is believed to cost around £1,500 a year on top of a joining fee of £750. Perhaps the doorman thought that five 'scruffy' youngsters would not be able to afford the club's prices.

After their world stadium tour announcement, the boys flew back to Europe to complete their current tour with their minds already set on the mammoth event to come next year. It would surely complete their steamrolling quest for world domination!

# Epilogue

The sweet smell of success was set to linger after One Direction launched their own fragrance, called Our Moment. Following in the footsteps of Justin Bieber, Lady Gaga, Taylor Swift, Britney Spears and Rihanna, the boys unveiled their scent for women at London's most iconic skyscraper, popularly known as the Gherkin.

The hexagonal bottle had an intricate crown lid which contained a mesh "pink flower", reflecting the colour of the contents. According to the official website, it was a "feminine fragrance … made up of splashes of fresh fruit and seasonal flowers infused with undertones of warm musk. The pink grapefruit, wild berries and redcurrants, combined with the delicacy of jasmine petals, and frangipani with the dry woody tones of musk and patchouli leave an enticing and playful scent on the skin."

Or, in Harry's, words, "It smells like a summer's day."

Liam sounded as though he might personally have collected the frangipani and patchouli plants, and infused the fragrance with their oils. "We love the idea behind a fragrance as you mix individual scents to create something so much better," he said. "To be honest with you we've never had so many meetings to make something. This is like a complicated piece of art. A lot of love went into this."

An excitable Niall (is he ever anything else?) was also eager to chip in about just how hands-on the process had been: "We worked hard to get it smelling just right," he said. "I've tested it on my family and they love it – and we can't wait to show it to our fans across the world." Then he added: "I had a little tester bottle and my mam is a big fan, so that's all my Christmas presents cleared up!"

The bottles, packed inside pink cardboard boxed bearing pictures of the five boys, were to be available in three sizes: 30ml at £21/$35 (US), 50ml at £29/$45 and 100ml at £39/$55. It was another clever marketing ploy to capitalise on their international recognition factor, and it was not to be sniffed at.

The five band members were also set to increase their bank balances by signing music publishing deals which enabled them to earn money on all songs they were credited for writing – paid individually rather than as a band.

As well as making money for themselves, they used their purchase power for various charitable causes, such as one to combat bullying in America. They teamed up with retail giant Office Depot to launch an education programme aimed at creating bully-free schools across America. It was a subject dear to Liam's heart, having suffered bullying himself as a youngster.

In the lead up to kids going back to school after the summer break, Office Depot sold One Direction-branded binders, notebooks and other stationery, with a portion of the proceeds from each sale funding an anti-bullying educational programme.

★   ★   ★

Meanwhile, back in the world of pop music, Harry assured everyone that he would never get fed up with the hysterical adulation. "I never get tired of the screaming girls," he said. "Do you know what, there's a lot of bands who get that for a bit and then it doesn't happen any more so I think we're very lucky that it still happens."

As well as having a personal chef on their world arena tour, their management also sent two mixed martial arts instructors from Leicester to help keep them fit: Mark Jarvis, who runs the Muscle Machine gym, and judo champion Jimmy Wallhead joined the boys as they entered the North American segment of their tour in June 2013. As well as regular workouts – including boxing, circuit training and low-carb diets – the boys were given a protein shake to help build up muscle.

He may look slim, but Zayn moaned that Niall was the only one who didn't really need to watch his weight. Despite having a seemingly insatiable appetite – and a love of junk food – he just didn't pile on the pounds.

"Niall is the skinniest. He just eats and eats and eats and eats, but he never puts any weight on," Zayn said to *Top Of The Pops* magazine. "It's a little bit annoying. The rest of us have to watch what we eat but Niall can eat just anything and be fine."

Zayn added that the band spend hours chatting about all sorts of trivial stuff and nonsense while on tour. "We talk so much rubbish. We just talk, talk, talk, talk," he commented. "We play games like PlayStation and we just do normal stuff like listen to music, watch movies and chill out. It depends on the mood we are in."

The comment was more enlightening than it at first appeared. It showed that, in the very eye of the raging tornado that was One Direction – sweeping up ever more screaming fans, awards, adulation and fame across the world – there remained five quite normal boys at heart, who still liked to spend their cherished downtime doing the same normal things as teenagers the whole world over.

# Thanks

I'd like to thank those people – both named and anonymous – who agreed to speak to me for this book. Your insights were of great interest.

And many thanks to commissioning editor David Barraclough at Omnibus for his patience and kindness and to copy editor Paul Woods for his efficiency and accuracy.

I could not have wished to have worked with anyone better.

Jim Maloney